"We know God is at work in this economic storm. Like other families, we must decide whether to throw our arms up in panic or trust Him and adjust to the changes around us. *Surviving Financial Meltdown* offers a road map to navigate the road we are on. Be teachable, gather the information, steady the course, and let Ron and Jeremy speak wisdom into your mind and heart as you continue to steward that which God has entrusted to you."

**Dr. Gary and Barb Rosberg**
America's Family Coaches
Cofounders, TheGreatMarriageExperience.com
Coauthors, *6 Secrets to a Lasting Love*

"How timely! Here's solid biblical advice on how to personally manage the 'uncertainty of riches' in a world that has gone into the dumper economically."

**Joe Stowell**
President, Cornerstone University
Grand Rapids, Michigan

"To be financially free is to know of God's provision . . . even in times of great economic uncertainty. Thank you, Ron and Jeremy, for helping us refocus on the practical, time-tested principles and truths of God's Word!"

**Jerry Black**
President, Legacy Planning Group, Inc.

"Ron Blue is a go-to guy in so many ways . . . as a leader, a counselor, a man of integrity, a friend, and a writer. That's why during these crazy and unpredictable financial times, he's once again my go-to guy for the principles my family and I need to survive!"

**Robert E. (Bob) Reccord**
President, Total Life Impact Ministries
Speaker, author, consultant

"Ron Blue and Jeremy White have done it again! Surviving tough economic challenges is nothing new, so the practical application of the biblical wisdom presented in this book is both timely and timeless. Prepare now—not just to survive, but to thrive."

**Janice A. Thompson, CFP**
President, Strategic Financial Solutions, Inc.

# SURVIVING
## Financial Meltdown
Confident Decisions in an Uncertain World

# RON BLUE

# JEREMY WHITE, CPA

Tyndale House Publishers, Inc.
Carol Stream, Illinois

Visit Tyndale's exciting Web site at www.tyndale.com

*TYNDALE* and Tyndale's quill logo are registered trademarks of Tyndale House Publishers, Inc.

Focus on the Family and the accompanying logo and design are trademarks of Focus on the Family, Colorado Springs, Colorado 80995.

*Surviving Financial Meltdown: Confident Decisions in an Uncertain World*

Copyright © 2009 by Ron Blue and Jeremy L. White. All rights reserved.

Cover photo copyright © by Steve McAlister/Getty Images. All rights reserved.

Designed by Jacqueline L. Nuñez

Edited by Kim Miller

Published in association with the literary agency of Wolgemuth & Associates, Inc.

Some material in chapters 5 and 7–9 is adapted from *Faith-Based Family Finances* (Carol Stream, IL: Tyndale House, 2008) by Ron Blue with Jeremy L. White.

All Scripture quotations, unless otherwise indicated, are taken from the HOLY BIBLE, NEW INTERNATIONAL VERSION®. NIV®. Copyright © 1973, 1978, 1984 by International Bible Society. Used by permission of Zondervan. All rights reserved.

Scripture quotations marked NKJV are taken from the New King James Version®. Copyright © 1982 by Thomas Nelson, Inc. Used by permission. All rights reserved. *NKJV* is a trademark of Thomas Nelson, Inc.

Scripture quotations marked NASB are taken from the *New American Standard Bible*®, copyright © 1960, 1962, 1963, 1968, 1971, 1972, 1973, 1975, 1977, 1995 by The Lockman Foundation. Used by permission.

**Library of Congress Cataloging-in-Publication Data**

Blue, Ron, date.
    Surviving financial meltdown : confident decisions in an uncertain world / Ron Blue and Jeremy L. White.
      p. cm.
    Includes bibliographical references.
    ISBN 978-1-4143-2995-6 (sc)
    1. Finance, Personal—Religious aspects—Christianity. I. White, Jeremy (Jeremy L.) II. Title.
    HG179.B5658 2009
    332.024—dc22                               2008048800

Printed in the United States of America

15   14   13   12   11   10   09
7    6    5    4    3    2    1

# CONTENTS

753

120573

## CHAPTER 1

# RIDING OUT THE ECONOMIC STORM
## How to Prepare for Economic Uncertainty

Plunging home values. Declining stock market. Vanishing credit. Fluctuating gas prices. Ongoing war against terrorism. Failing banks. Soaring food costs. Falling value of the dollar. Swelling budget deficits. (Suggested cover story for the next *Money* magazine: "Best Investment Now: Antacids!")

If you're worried, you're not alone. You're not the only one feeling the uncertainty. Consumer confidence measurements have reached their lowest level in decades.

Most of the world would still leap at the chance to trade economic situations with you. You realize that. But you're still nervous and searching for answers.

It's easy enough to present our case that economic times are challenging. The daily headlines back us up on that. Our challenge in this book is to prepare you so that you have less fear and more financial peace.

We want to help you develop a commonsense financial strategy to weather the economic storms of today as well as those in the far-off financial future. In times of economic uncertainty, the strength of your strategy will determine whether you thrive or survive.

Let's get started with a reminder of how you get ready for tough times: Prepare in advance.

## Don't Let Your Dreams Be Washed Away

The aerial photo is startling: An attractively designed yellow two-story home stands alone on highly sought-after real estate along the Texas Gulf Coast. Just a few days before, that house was part of a thriving community. Now, it is surrounded on every side by the wreckage of about 200 other homes and buildings. A private helicopter pilot, flying over the area after it had been slammed by Hurricane Ike in September 2008, took the photo.

Not long after the pilot posted the image on CNN's iReport site, the buzz started. Viewers began debating whether the photo was a fake. After all, how could one home withstand 110 mph winds and a storm surge while every other building around it had been pulverized? The speculation ended when the sister of one of the home's owners identified it and provided another photo of the house taken just a few months earlier.

Reporters quickly located the home's owners, Warren and Pam Adams. Just three years before, the Adamses' home had been destroyed by Hurricane Rita. Because they loved the beach, the couple wanted to rebuild rather than leave the coast. So they did—but with the knowledge that their new home might also be in the path of a hurricane someday.

The couple hired an engineering firm to oversee the contractor as their new residence was built. The builder put the house's bottom floor on wooden columns that raised it above the surrounding houses. The foundation was made with reinforced concrete, and builders followed the latest hurricane building codes to the letter.

Despite its solid construction, the home did sustain some damage in Hurricane Ike. The first-floor garage and a wooden staircase on the home's exterior were destroyed. The interior suffered water and mud damage, and furniture, appliances, and other possessions were ruined. Yet unlike their neighbors, who returned to their former home sites hoping to find a few personal belongings among the rubble, the Adamses can repair their home.

The precautions the couple took when rebuilding their home after Hurricane Rita may have seemed extreme to some. Yet their foresight appears brilliant now, after the town sustained a direct hit by Hurricane Ike. In fact, after Aaron Reed, a spokesman with the Texas Parks and Wildlife Department, confirmed that the Adamses' home was the only surviving home on that side of the beach, he added, "I thought, if I were ever to build a house on the coast, I'm going to contact the guy who built this."[1]

---

## AMERICANS' TOP 5 PERSONAL FINANCIAL FEARS

**1. Rising cost of living.** When asked about their greatest financial fears, about two-thirds of respondents said they were "very worried" about inflation; another 30 percent said they were "somewhat worried." A majority said they were concerned their salaries won't keep up with rising food, gasoline, health care, and other costs. More than a third admitted that they worried because their housing costs consume at least half their household income.

**2. The economic downturn and job insecurity.** Nearly 90 percent worried about recession, and almost 40 percent were concerned about job layoffs. Nearly two-thirds worried about stock market declines.

**3. Consumer debt.** Over 60 percent of respondents who carry credit card debt from month to month worried that they have too much. A significant percentage of respondents were also troubled by the amount of student loan debt, medical debt, home equity debt, and lines of credit they carry.

**4. The housing crisis.** More than half were worried about falling home prices and the loss of equity in their homes. About one-quarter of homeowners polled were somewhat or very worried they could face foreclosure. Another 45 percent worried that rising property taxes could force them from their homes. Half expressed concern because their homes require basic maintenance or repairs they can't afford.

**5. Savings.** Nearly 60 percent worried because they have nothing saved for retirement and can't afford to save. Another one-third were worried they have nothing saved for future college expenses.

According to a poll of 2,000 adults conducted by Decipher, Inc., and Yahoo! Finance in July 2008. See http://finance.yahoo.com/expert/article/moneyhappy/95501.

---

In fact, the couple simply displayed common sense. They knew that their home had been destroyed once by a hurricane and that it could happen again. Of course, others along the Gulf Coast knew they faced that threat as well. The difference was in how they responded to that risk.

Like some Gulf Coast residents, many people today build their financial houses without much of a strategy. When you build something you want to keep, common sense dictates that you build it according to a plan and with materials that will last. This strategy works for all types of construction, from putting together a financial portfolio to building a house.

Warren and Pam Adams can't prevent a hurricane from smashing into their home on the coastline. They can't control which way the wind blows. They can, however, build their house to withstand the wind and water.

## Mr. Blue Goes to Washington

Palms sweating and heart racing, I (Ron) climbed the granite steps of the Capitol building to testify as an expert witness before a Senate subcommittee. I entered the chamber room where the hearings took place. I had often seen it on television. It was impressive yet intimidating. The senators were seated higher than the witness table and the visitors' gallery.

I recognized many of the senators' names on the plaques at their table and took a deep breath. I reminded myself that I wasn't in trouble—even though the room had the feel of a courtroom. The Senate subcommittee was holding hearings on "Solutions for the New Era: Jobs and Families." I was one of several "experts" from various economic and social fields. Other participants on the panel pressed for more social programs.

When my turn to speak came, I was hoping my voice wouldn't crack. Could I live up to my introduction as a financial expert? Leaning in toward the microphone on the table, I began to answer a senator's question about what the average American family should do in the current economy. I said I believed the American family could benefit from following a four-part financial plan:

1. Think long-term with goals and investing
2. Spend less than they earn
3. Maintain liquidity (or emergency savings)
4. Minimize the use of debt

The Senate chamber room fell silent for a moment. I was expecting laughter to reverberate among the marble columns and high ceiling at the simplicity of what I had said. The committee chairman, Christopher Dodd, looked down at his notes. He furrowed his brow and pursed his lips. He recited the points back to me. Instead of chuckling at me, he then said, "It seems like this plan is not just for the family. It seems it would work at any income level."

"Yes," I replied with some relief. Now I was the one doing a bit of chuckling as I added, "including the U.S. government." We went on to have an engaging conversation about how the senators could exercise strong leadership through wise financial practices.

## Four Principles of Financial Success

I had developed my four-part answer to the senator's question over many years. In fact, I have heard that same question over and over. After a presentation to a large audience or in response to a call-in radio program, people often ask how to get out of a financial mess—or avoid one. Often the questioners hope that I'll provide an instant solution for their financial difficulties. Though they may be disappointed to hear my commonsense strategy, I know this time-tested, biblically supported answer works.

Let's briefly expand our explanation of these principles here:

*Think long term.* The longer term your perspective, the better financial decisions you'll make. Set goals in writing for the future. Invest for the long term and worry less about short-term ups and downs in your 401(k) or investment portfolio.

*Spend less than you earn.* To accomplish this, you need to know what you're earning and what you're spending. Make a spending plan (or, if we dare use that loathed term, a budget). Monitor how you're doing. Develop the self-control to avoid over-spending. If you consistently spend less than you earn over a long period of time, you will do well financially.

*Maintain emergency savings.* A reserve set aside will help you ride out the surprises life throws at you. You must spend less than you earn to build savings. Savings will then help you avoid debt. These principles work together.

*Minimize the use of debt.* Debt increases risk. It may allow you to do more or have more now, but debt will reduce your ability to have more in the future. I know of few cases of financial disaster occurring without debt. Financial problems are magnified with debt.

These four financial principles are so simple that they may easily be overlooked. Yet they have stood the test of time. They work when the economy is in a recession or depression, or in boom times. They work despite inflation or deflation. They apply when gas prices or real estate values are rising or falling. They were outlined thousands of years ago in the Bible. Many rich people—and many poor people—can attest to their truths.

Some technical professionals, such as doctors and engineers, initially think these principles are too simplistic. They want to make succeeding financially as technically challenging and sophisticated as their fields. But you can't go wrong if you follow these steps. What kind of financial trouble would you ever get in if you spent less than you earned, minimized debt, kept savings available, and thought about the long term?

6

## When Do I Apply These Principles?

Warren and Pam Adams prepared for possible disaster *before* it happened. The best time to apply these four steps is *before* the financial storms come.

You may be thinking, *Well, it's too late for that. I'm in the midst of a financial crisis. The hurricane has already hit. Now what do I do?* Here's hope. You start with these four principles of financial success. If you haven't done them before, then start now. You can't lay a solid financial foundation without these four steps. They will lead you out of a crisis—and prevent many future ones.

Perhaps your financial crisis has already happened. You may have lost your job. You may be getting calls from creditors. Perhaps you fear a possible foreclosure. You're picking up the

---

### 8 STEPS TO TAKE IF YOUR JOB SEEMS IN JEOPARDY

1. Talk with your manager about your concerns (no sense worrying unnecessarily).

2. Look for ways to make yourself more valuable to your employer, perhaps by learning a skill (e.g., a computer program or language) that will set you apart from your coworkers.

3. Update your résumé.

4. Secure references while still with your current employer.

5. Network with your professional and personal contacts, asking them to pass along job leads and information about various companies and industries, and to introduce you to other professionals who might help during a future job search—and then reciprocate whenever possible. Keep a log detailing each contact and the feedback you receive.

6. Check want ads and job boards on the Internet regularly for openings in your field.

7. Redirect discretionary spending into your emergency fund.

8. Find a prayer partner or partners.

---

pieces and trying to rebuild. What do you do? Same answer. You start with these principles.

Perhaps you don't currently face a financial crisis but are anxious because of all the economic bad news. The Adamses' house is a great illustration that may motivate you to prepare for storms in advance. You can take great comfort in these transcendent principles that apply before, during, and after the crisis.

In fact, some positive results can come from our country's current economic downturn. We've learned that a crisis can sharpen our focus. It helps us think more rationally. When gas prices rose significantly, consumers started moving from large sport-utility vehicles and oversized trucks to more fuel-efficient vehicles. This is rational. But even when gas was less expensive, was a Hummer ever a sensible purchase for an urban dweller?

People often ask us, "Now that _____ [you fill in the blank] is happening, what should I do?" We always give the same advice: follow these four principles. If you set long-term goals and invest accordingly, if you spend less than your income, if you have available savings, and if you reduce debt, then you'll be as prepared as possible.

## No Surprise Ending with This Book— But Keep Reading

We suppose this would make a poor novel. No mystery or suspense here. We've already revealed the four principles of financial success and told you the ending of the story.

However, we hope you haven't missed the paradox: these principles are easy to understand, but they're often hard to do. We've stated the principles but not yet helped you understand how you can begin doing them. In the coming chapters, we'll explore these principles in greater detail. You'll discover how to approach the future—any future—with financial peace of mind.

We realize that it's not just a matter of following four simple steps in a vacuum. You're part of an overall economy. You can't avoid feeling some of the effects of our nation's economic downturn—but it doesn't have to be as great as you fear. You hear things that make you anxious. Money issues carry with them emotions, baggage from the past, and uncertainty about the future. You probably don't have a degree in financial management. When it comes to handling your own money, you may be in unfamiliar territory. So we're going to begin by exploring what causes financial fears in our economy. Then you'll identify your particular fears.

You can do this. You can learn to manage your finances wisely. It's not too late. Reading financial how-tos is like exercising or eating healthy food. You know you're supposed to, but will you do it? Go for it. People with less education, less talent, less income than you have done it. Financial peace of mind can be more than just a future hope. It can be your expectation. In the pages ahead, you will learn how to take this expectation and make it a reality in your life.

## CHAPTER 2

# THIS ECONOMY IS UNIQUE, JUST LIKE EVERY OTHER ONE BEFORE IT
## Dealing with a Challenging Economy

Perhaps it's a sign of the times? Starbucks is feeling the effects of the economic slowdown. After rapid growth in the 2000s, the high-end coffee retailer announced plans not long ago to close hundreds of stores and cut as many as 12,000 jobs worldwide. Consumers appear to be altering their habits when a latte costs about as much as a gallon of milk.[2] Chief operating executive Howard Schultz said customers are "visiting us less frequently as a result of economic pressures."[3]

Economic pressure, he calls it. So that's what you feel in your head before taking another aspirin. It's easy to see why people feel squeezed. Rising fuel prices and food costs on one end, falling stock values and home prices on the other. Take a look at that lemon on your restaurant table after using it to flavor your water. Squeezed, twisted, pulp hanging out—nothing left to give except a bit of a sour taste. That's how you may feel in our economy now.

Trends indicate you're not alone. The use of discount coupons declined every year since 1992 but is now rising again. In the summer of 2008, the humble, entry-level Toyota Corolla became the best-selling vehicle in the United States, taking the spot held for more than two decades by the large Ford F-150 pickup.[4]

## Been There, Done That, Bought the T-Shirt

What's going to happen? Will we make it through the tough times? Such uncertainty. We don't like it. We want to know where we stand. Many people have told us, "I just want a little security."

The first step in defeating uncertainty is to realize just how common it is. It's normal. Economic uncertainty is certain. There's nothing new under the sun.

Think of these headlines: "Sudden Spike in Oil Prices Causing Angst." "Unrest Continues in the Middle East." "Congressional Action Likely on Windfall Profit Tax." Were these written during the 1973 oil embargo? Or in 1979 after the Iranian Revolution? Or in 2008? The answer is D: All of the above.

You might think these headlines are from the early 2000s: "Soaring New Economy Stocks Go Bust." "Corporate Corruption Scandals Threaten Market Integrity." Actually, these describe the situation in the 1870s after the railroad stocks, which had been market darlings promising a new future, derailed. Corruption among publicly owned companies in that decade caused many investors to lose much of their investments.

We have lived through cycles of difficult economic circumstances. I (Ron) can remember being fearful as I was building a financial planning firm in the early 1980s. Interest rates were nearing 20 percent, inflation was raging, and the stock market had been flat for several years. The gloom-and-doom forecasters said that this was how the U.S. economy would continue to operate and that Japan would overtake us. I was afraid they were right. It seemed like there was no way to make a sensible financial plan work in that environment.

After the terrorist attacks on the United States in 2001, the stock market closed for nearly a week; the political situation was unstable. Some doomsayers predicted the global economy would be in shambles. I (Jeremy) remember advising clients to stick with their long-term investment perspective during those three dismal stock market years from 2000 to 2002. It was difficult even for me to have such confidence in scary times. Yet the stock market increased the next five years.

The doomsayers and the fearful clients were wrong. The economy recovered. What happened at the end of that negative economic cycle? A positive one began. Again. Just like every time before.

## Get a Grip!

Whether it's Y2K fears, stock market declines, or subprime mortgage problems, various doomsayers will crawl out and attract listeners with their dire predictions. Doomsayers have a depression mentality. But they are unwilling to take depression actions. If they really believed that a depression were coming, they would get out of debt, convert all their investments to government securities and gold, buy a one-year supply of food, and otherwise prepare for the worst. Although people like to talk about and believe that an extreme situation will happen, very few are willing to take extreme steps to prepare for it.

During our years as financial advisors, we didn't believe in implementing plans for the extremes. Planning for extremes usually dictates radical action. Radical actions can have radical consequences. Many well-intentioned people have thought the economy would collapse or that the political systems would crumble. Someday, someone may get lucky and guess close to the right time. In the meantime, we suggest pursuing balanced practicality.

In the book we wrote with the late Larry Burkett called *Your Money after the Big 5-0: Money Essentials for the Second Half of Life*, we provided five realities (or truths) to help people thrive despite a slippery, sliding economy (see the sidebar on page 14). You can apply these five realities to your own situation, giving you balanced practicality as you make financial decisions.

## 5 ECONOMIC REALITIES FOR TOUGH TIMES

**1. Economies and stock markets go up and down.** So . . .
> *Do* plan for and expect downturns.
> *Don't* sell low and buy high based on emotion, or fret about periodic declines that show up on your statements.

**2. The only certainty is uncertainty.** So . . .
> *Do* expect change and look for the opportunities it brings.
> *Don't* worry, avoid risks because of fear, or attempt to control events.

**3. The conventional wisdom is usually wrong.** So . . .
> *Do* seek wisdom from God as you pray and study Scripture; seek godly counsel from others.
> *Don't* look for "insider secrets" to success; don't avoid counsel offered by knowledgeable friends and professionals.

**4. No one investment works every time.** So . . .
> *Do* diversify to spread out your risk.
> *Don't* stop investing.

**5. Correct principles work correctly throughout time.** So . . .
> *Do* remain calm even in financial storms.
> *Don't* let fear or lack of confidence keep you from sticking to solid financial plans.

## Biblical Perspective—Always Right, Relevant, and Unchanging

Where can you go to find timeless wisdom about handling your finances? Look no further than the Bible. Scripture specifically tells us that wealth and the economy are uncertain—something borne out by current economic difficulties. Consider this wisdom Paul passed on to Timothy:

> *Command those who are rich in this present world not to be arrogant nor to put their hope in wealth, which is so uncertain, but to put their hope in God, who richly provides us with everything for our enjoyment.*
> 1 Timothy 6:17

Do you see the first absolute in this verse? Simply stated, wealth is uncertain. Your retirement plan, your dollars in the bank, your job, your real estate—all of your wealth. It's uncertain. Don't be shocked into a frenzied panic when it goes up and down. Don't borrow continually assuming your wealth is certain. It's not. Volatility should be no surprise because your wealth is uncertain.

Then, look at the contrast in this verse. Don't put your hope in uncertain wealth. Put your hope in God. He promises to provide what we need. Paul is pointing toward God's certainty. Here's another passage that does it more pointedly. When the financial crises hit and it looks like no institution can be trusted, We like to be reminded of this passage:

> *Find rest, O my soul, in God alone;*
> *my hope comes from him.*
> *He alone is my rock and my salvation;*
> *he is my fortress, I will not be shaken.*
> *My salvation and my honor depend on God;*
> *he is my mighty rock, my refuge.*
> *Trust in him at all times, O people;*
> *pour out your hearts to him,*
> *for God is our refuge.* Psalm 62:5-8

## Use Your Noise-Canceling Headphones

Have you ever boarded an airplane planning to finish a report for work, dive into a best seller, or catch up on your sleep? Were you immediately distracted by a wailing baby or an animated conversation between your seatmates? If so, the most useful item on that airplane might have been noise-canceling headphones. Once you put those on, the outside noises were muffled. Though you might not understand the acoustical physics of how they work, the earphones helped you concentrate or nap.

After you had them on for a while, you became used to the quieter atmosphere. But if you took the headphones off, everything around you seemed even more loud and bothersome than before.

Financial fear and stress can rise with so much "noise" in our economy. It often seems that the goal of the media is to make you fearful. Fearful analysts, worried politicians, anxious bloggers, and shrieking talk show hosts are scared about all sorts of things—especially about the future!

You hear the announcer on your favorite radio news station saying, "Unemployment rose to 6.1 percent and jobless claims increased by 20,000 over last month." Useless noise. It sounds unnerving because no context is given. The news reporter doesn't tell you that 6.1 percent unemployment is still much lower than during the last four recessions. Or that jobless claims usually rise in the colder months because of slowing construction.

When the stock market goes down 200 points, the headline is bigger in the newspaper than when it goes up 200 points. Distracting noise.

The TV anchor says on Friday that the market ended the week on a bad note by dropping 150 points. She doesn't tell you that it went up 50 points each day from Monday to Thursday. She doesn't emphasize that it ended the week higher. Chalkboard-scratching noise.

Our advice is to put on your imaginary noise-canceling headphones. Muffle the day-to-day noise. You can do this in several ways: Stay focused on your goals and situation. Read truths in God's Word more often than the newspaper. Avoid

---

### 4 THINGS TO DO IF YOU'VE HEARD YOUR BANK MAY FAIL

1. Make sure your accounts are below the maximum amount insured by the FDIC (currently $250,000).

2. Move emergency savings to another bank.

3. Check your bank's rating on Bankrate.com, http://www.bankrate.com/brm/safesound/ss_home.asp.

4. Keep a higher level of cash on hand.

the distractions. Don't be convinced that everyone is fearful and you should be too.

Advertisers also tap into this "shouldn't you be worried?" line of thinking. They want you uncomfortable enough, discontented enough, to buy their product or service. Just consider this commercial: A father and daughter are having a picnic in a tranquil park, sitting by a stream. He's relaxing under the tree. She's staring off in the distance as butterflies flutter nearby.

The father asks, "What are you thinking about, honey?"

"Butterflies," the young girl sweetly says. "What are you thinking about, Daddy?"

"I'm thinking about butterflies too," he responds, smiling contentedly.

"But, Daddy," the girl says very seriously as she turns to him, "aren't you worried about protecting your company and employees in the changing global economy?"

The father furrows his brow as she moves toward him. "Are you tapped into the right capital market expertise to help manage your institutional assets?"

She's in his face now. "And, Daddy, what about life insurance? college? retirement? You need a smart financial plan, you know."

The message: adults—be worried. The unique twist of this commercial is that it's the child reminding her father to be worried about financial matters. Perhaps it's a good reminder if you haven't addressed certain financial matters. But if you're following a sound strategy—it's just more noise.

By the way, we can't help telling you the end of the commercial. The father says, "We are with AIG, honey. So I'm just thinking about butterflies."

The daughter replies, "Oh," and returns to playing.

The narrator then intones, "AIG—the strength to be there."

Ironically, in September 2008, AIG was rescued by a federal bridge loan when the company was teetering on the edge of bankruptcy, providing another reminder of the truth in Psalm

62. Financial institutions come and go and need to be bailed out. God is your fortress and cannot be shaken.

## Remember the Most Important Economic Indicator

When trying to gauge the overall economy, economists look at economic indicators. These include new building permits, manufacturers' orders, and new applications for unemployment. Bureaucrats track these numbers, politicians quote them to support their policies, and business analysts try to predict the future from them. Economists and pundits often refer to the Index of Leading Indicators, calculated according to 10 key economic variables to estimate future economic activity.

I (Ron) was recently interviewed by a host of a personal finance radio program. The host described recent economic trends and statistics. He then turned to me and asked, "What do you think is the most important economic indicator?"

I replied, "For me, it's my checkbook balance." This brought a few laughs, but I was serious. The global economy and all the various economic indicators aren't as important to my personal and financial well-being as the cash flow into my account, the cash flow out, and the cash availability.

## Are You a Thermometer or Thermostat?

The economic upheaval caused by problems such as real estate weakness, the federal budget deficit, and stock market corrections can create a climate of tension, anxiety, and fear. People tend to respond to this environment in one of two ways: they either behave like thermometers or like thermostats.

"Thermometers" respond to mounting fear and uncertainty with a jump in their emotional mercury. When the red line shoots up, suddenly even routine tasks can seem difficult. Small obstacles become big ones. Fear takes hold. Their instinct is to moan, cry, or collapse in a puddle of ineffectiveness. When the situation stabilizes, their mercury recedes.

They regain a sense of control—at least until the next crisis appears.

Often, that crisis is only as far away as the next headline. Thermometers reflect their environments. They react to and are at the mercy of an ever-changing climate.

"Thermostats," on the other hand, control their temperature. They manage their environments and keep working toward their goals of the target temperature. In other words, they keep their focus fixed on their long-term goals, they spend less than they earn, they continue building savings, and they work hard to get out of debt.

I (Ron) remember seeing a former client at a holiday party. He wrapped his arms around me in a giant bear hug and said, with tears in his eyes, "I just want to thank you!"

"For what?" I asked.

"Michigan is in the midst of some really tough economic times," he began, describing a situation I knew to be true. But I wasn't sure why he was thanking me.

Several years ago my friend had launched his own business. Driven by a fear of failure and the desire to accumulate wealth, he steered the company to apparent success—borrowing heavily to do so. As Michigan slid into recession, my friend nearly lost it all. Tumbling real estate prices coupled with escalating interest rates and inflation left him riddled with fear about the future.

As he greeted me at the party, however, he did not look frightened. In fact, he looked happy. Yet I knew he was accurate in saying Michigan's economy was struggling.

"I don't know what's ahead," he explained. "Things will probably get worse, but I'm not worried. In fact, I'm actually looking forward to the future!"

I recalled that when my friend had contacted me after his initial scare, I had worked with him to develop a plan that would allow him to get out of debt, build liquidity into his financial situation, and significantly increase his charitable giving. Now, my friend was eager to witness the strength of his financial strategy under pressure. He had carefully positioned himself in such a way that he would not only survive during difficult economic times, he would thrive. He's a thermostat.

My friend is not a one-in-a-million success story. Instead he represents a financial position that is possible for you. You don't have to react to your changing financial climate in a knee-jerk or haphazard fashion. You can become a thermostat, affecting your individual environment through proper planning and preparation. You can thrive during economic uncertainty. This should be not merely your desire but your expectation—regardless of the financial forecast.

In 2007, Tony Dungy, head coach of the Indianapolis Colts and the first African American coach to win a Super Bowl, earned a spot on the Time 100, a list of the 100 most influential Americans compiled by *Time* magazine.[5] What is the secret to Dungy's success? He's been lauded for his quiet, resolute approach to coaching, which is often at odds with the loud, intimidating demeanor of most pro football coaches.

Yet another key to his success comes from Dungy himself. He says, "Things will go wrong at times. You can't always control circumstances. However, you can always control your attitude, approach, and response. Your options are to complain or to look ahead and figure out how to make the situation better."[6]

The wisdom in Dungy's strategy may be applied in any arena, from football to finances. You have no individual control over what happens with national real estate prices. You can't influence inflation or guess which way the stock market is going. Economic conditions are always changing and out of your control, but biblical principles are unchanging. When facing economic uncertainty, use the biblical principles to your advantage.

We've tried to help you tune out the usual sources of economic worry. You may think that this chapter neglected your deeply held fears. We know your specific fears can be real and frightening. In the next chapter, we'll help you pinpoint your fears, deal with them, and put them into perspective.

## CHAPTER 3

# NO SENSE BEING PESSIMISTIC—
# IT WOULDN'T WORK ANYWAY!
### Dealing with Your Financial Fears

Tonya Macklin, a single mom who works two jobs, was interviewed by a *USA Today* reporter in fall 2008 about the stress she feels over her finances. The Boston-area resident had lost her home a year earlier because she could no longer afford the payments, and then filed for bankruptcy protection. Soon after, she was hospitalized for exhaustion.

As she considers the future for herself and her ten-year-old daughter, Macklin is weighed down by fear. In fact, she admits to having trouble sleeping at night. "I just put it in God's hands. I go to bed praying each night that things will someday get better."[7]

I'd be willing to bet that on those nights when Macklin tosses and turns in her bed, she is not agonizing over the latest federal budget deficit or inflation figures. She doesn't care about tax code changes or Japan's stock market. Instead she's focused on the specifics of her own precarious financial situation.

We have all wrestled with our own private worries and personal fears. In the last chapter we examined how to respond to large-scale economic changes. Now we want to shift the focus to your concerns. Personal fears, desires, and long-range dreams often create an anxiety far outweighing the noise of the national economic news.

21

## 6 INCREDIBLE PROMISES FROM GOD
## TO REMEMBER IN TOUGH TIMES

1. *Yet I am always with you; you hold me by my right hand. You guide me with your counsel, and afterward you will take me into glory. Whom have I in heaven but you? And earth has nothing I desire besides you. My flesh and my heart may fail, but God is the strength of my heart and my portion forever.* (Psalm 73:23-26)

2. *Though the fig tree does not bud and there are no grapes on the vines, though the olive crop fails and the fields produce no food, though there are no sheep in the pen and no cattle in the stalls, yet I will rejoice in the LORD, I will be joyful in God my Savior. The Sovereign LORD is my strength; he makes my feet like the feet of a deer, he enables me to go on the heights.* (Habakkuk 3:17-19)

3. *Do not worry, saying, "What shall we eat?" or "What shall we drink?" or "What shall we wear?" For the pagans run after all these things, and your heavenly Father knows that you need them. But seek first his kingdom and his righteousness, and all these things will be given to you as well.* (Matthew 6:31-33)

4. *Therefore we do not lose heart. Though outwardly we are wasting away, yet inwardly we are being renewed day by day. For our light and momentary troubles are achieving for us an eternal glory that far outweighs them all. So we fix our eyes not on what is seen, but on what is unseen. For what is seen is temporary, but what is unseen is eternal.* (2 Corinthians 4:16-18)

5. *Do not be anxious about anything, but in everything, by prayer and petition, with thanksgiving, present your requests to God. And the peace of God, which transcends all understanding, will guard your hearts and your minds in Christ Jesus.* (Philippians 4:6-7)

6. *Keep your lives free from the love of money and be content with what you have, because God has said, "Never will I leave you; never will I forsake you."* (Hebrews 13:5)

## Avoiding the Eeyore Syndrome

We live in an imperfect world full of imperfect people. Life is messy. Surprises happen. Think, for a brief and somewhat unpleasant moment, of how much and how quickly life can go awry: a sick child, bankruptcy of a business, divorce, layoff, nursing home stay, lawsuit, damage to your reputation, or disability.

How do you respond to the unexpected events of life that directly and indirectly affect your personal finances? Our fears, desires, and dreams are often entirely valid. Yet the emotional punch they pack need not be a knockout blow. In this chapter you'll learn to admit to and identify the specific concerns that threaten your personal financial security. You will gain a perspective on your financial future that will become the foundation for your ultimate money-management program.

A few years ago, Rick and Denise seemed to have everything. They had recently semiretired and moved to their dream home, which the couple had designed together. It is 50 steps away from the 10th hole of a country club's golf course, and the interior includes cathedral ceilings, stereo speakers in every room, and a hot tub adjacent to the master bedroom.

Yet when their investment portfolio took a big hit, Rick was forced to return to work and now oversees leasing at a car dealership in Medina, Ohio. Recently the couple made another tough decision: they decided to put their home on the market. "We cried over it," says Rick. "It was a very emotional decision."[8]

Years ago I (Ron) knew a family who lived in a nice section of Atlanta with five healthy, active children. The father, a man in his early 40s, loved spending time with his kids.

One weekend he took the older children hiking in the North Carolina mountains. Climbing up a seemingly safe path beside a waterfall, he grabbed a tree branch. The branch broke. The father lost his balance and plummeted to his death on the rocks below.

How was his wife to cope with rearing five children on her own? In addition to the emotional loss, her financial concerns must have seemed staggering. Could she count on her family and friends? Perhaps. But her deceased husband's business partner was another matter. He sued to get a bigger share of the business. How do you prepare for something like that?

### Desires: The Goals You Yearn to Achieve

Failing to reach your desires may not be as devastating as realizing your fears. Yet your desires, which may include things like getting out of debt, taking a vacation, buying a house, purchasing a better car, or providing for a child's higher-education bills are also real causes of anxiety.

Many of our dreams—in fact, the American Dream itself—seem to be vanishing into an early-morning fog. So many of the things we once took for granted suddenly appear out of reach. Is it still reasonable to hope, as our parents did, that at some point we will no longer have a home mortgage? Owning your own home used to be considered almost a right; now it seems more like a privilege.

The same may be said of a college education. According to the College Board, the average annual cost for a private college is $30,367 for tuition, room, and board. That's right—per year. The four-year total is $121,468. That's today—not years from now. The average annual cost at a four-year public university is $12,796.[9] And the skyrocketing costs show no sign of slowing. Suddenly, putting your children—or yourself—through college is no longer something to be taken for granted.

### Long-Range Dreams: More Distant Now than Ever Before?

Further away—but still real—are the hopes and dreams that make for long-term planning. A desire to launch your own business, increase your charitable giving, or gain the financial independence necessary for retirement may be longer-term goals.

Investment counselors urge their clients to get serious about planning. Clients tend to procrastinate. As a slogan for a mutual fund company once warned: "Planning for retirement is like trying to hit a moving target blindfolded."

So what are we to do? Throw in the investment towel and simply cross our fingers? Start buying lottery tickets in bulk?

## 7 WEB SITES TO VISIT FOR HELPFUL PERSONAL FINANCE RESOURCES

1. www.masteryourmoney.com

2. www.mymoney.gov

3. www.crown.org

4. www.360financialliteracy.org/Life+Stages

5. www.blythewhite.com (select "Investment Services" and then "Calculators" under the "Research" menu to find helpful financial calculators)

6. www.wiserwomen.org

7. www.focusonthefamily.com (select "Life Challenges" and then "Managing Money")

Hope that rich Uncle Frank will go before we do and pray that we will get at least some of the inheritance?

Most people desperately need an effective plan for retirement. Relying on Social Security alone is not enough. In September 2008, the average monthly benefit received by American workers was a meager $995[10]—an income scarcely above the poverty level for people older than 65. And that figure is likely to drop as the Social Security system adds more and more retirees to its roster—many of whom will live at least 10 to 20 years longer than their counterparts of the 1920s and 1930s. Average Social Security payments have increased each year but have risen more slowly than medical costs have increased.

The challenge you face in planning for retirement (or for other long-term dreams) can generate a great deal of tension and anxiety. The fear that you might not realize your hopes and desires may prove just as unsettling as the threat of an unexpected loss or crisis. Yet none of these fears should compromise your peace of mind. Confront your fears head-on, wrestling them into submission before they become a stronghold in your life.

## Pinpointing Your Fears

To conquer the negative emotions stirred up by your circumstances, you must first admit to and then specifically identify your fears.

*Admit your fears.* The first step in overcoming financial fear is to acknowledge it. It's not sinful or wrong to experience fear, doubt, or uncertainty. Neither is it uncommon.

You can't hide your head in the sand. Refusing to see or acknowledge your fear will not make it go away. In fact, if left to fester, it will probably grow to new and more frightening proportions. Admit you are afraid—and then move on to tackle your fear.

*Identify your fears.* The second vital step in conquering fear is to identify it. Once you admit that you are experiencing fear, you must label your specific concerns. A correct diagnosis of the problem is essential to discovering the proper cure.

Take a few moments to mentally catalog your financial fears. Do any of the following items threaten your sense of security? Review the list, marking any areas that reflect your individual concerns.

## Catalog of Fears
_____A. Past Mistakes

Financially, if you could do one thing over, what would it be?

_____

_____

_____

Are there other financial mistakes you have made that are creating anxiety right now?

_____

_____

_____

____**B. Future Dreams, Desires, Goals, Opportunities**
____Children's education
____Personal education
____Retirement
____Financial independence
____Starting your own business
____Purchasing first or new home
____Paying off debt
____Other_____

____**C. Future Uncertainties, Challenges, or Fears**
____Death of a loved one, causing personal financial
       hardship
____Loss of a job
____Medical/health/accident-related concerns
____Long-term care event/Alzheimer's disease
____Business failure
____Investment losses
____Other_____

____**D. External forces**
____Job security
____Terrorist attacks
____The national economy
____Technology changes
____Other_____

Fear and faith don't mix well. Faith should overrule fear. Having pinpointed your specific fears, work through the following steps to deal with your concerns. (Hint: If you can't confidently answer all the questions in this section, come back and complete this page when you finish reading this book.)

**Dealing with Your Fears**
A. Of all the fears you identified and checked, cross off those that are out of your control.

B. Of those that are left, identify your top two fears:
   1. _____
   2. _____
C. How likely is it that number 1 will occur? _____ percent
   chance
   How likely is it that number 2 will occur? _____ percent
   chance
D. If number 1 does occur, what is the estimated financial cost?
   $ _____
   If number 2 does occur, what is the estimated financial cost?
   $ _____
E. What steps can you take to prepare for these outcomes?
   1. _____
   2. _____
   3. _____
   4. _____
   5. _____

Admitting and identifying your specific concerns is the first step to dealing with the fear of uncertainty. Don't just carry a load of hazy, general fears around in your head. Writing them down often makes them manageable. It enables you to confront real issues proactively.

## Do I Seem Self-Centered, or Is It Just Me?

As a financial advisor, I (Ron) have found that people wrestle with two primary fears: the fear of failure and the fear of the future. Psychologists would likely equate the fear of failure with our search for significance, while the fear of the future represents our search for security. In terms of financial planning, our thinking often runs along these lines: *If I have enough wealth, I will be secure (or significant or both).*

Let me use my personal experience as an example of the fear of failure. I grew up in a modest home with parents who never went to college. After becoming a teenager, I stepped from an eighth-grade class of only 12 students into a high school where there were 600 students in my class alone. I desperately wanted to be "someone," and by the time I graduated, I had lettered in two sports, served as senior-class president, and achieved the distinction I craved.

I continued to make a name for myself in college and then went on to pass the CPA exam on my first try. Later I acquired my MBA degree and got a job with the world's largest accounting firm.

To an outside observer, my life appeared to be woven with the threads of success. I typically worked seventy- to eighty-hour weeks, relying on my accumulating wealth to give me a feeling of significance and success. What I did not realize, however, was that a fear of failure dictated my every move.

Once I committed my life to Christ, nothing changed in terms of my controlling fears. I still worked more than seventy hours a week, this time for the "cause of Christ." I thrived on the recognition I received from the Christian community, and my reputation as a hardworking, dedicated Christian brought me immense satisfaction. It reached the point where, in my mind, it seemed that the church—if not the Lord Himself—was somehow dependent on my outstanding efforts.

Finally a friend pointed out that, as a Christian, I was allowing myself to be driven by the very same force that had influenced my lifestyle in the secular world. The fear of failure was just as wrong in the one arena as in the other, with consequences equally as adverse.

My fear of failure (or search for significance) is typically more of a male issue than a female one. Men, more often than women, tend to be driven by the fear that if they don't push hard enough or work long enough, they will fail. Often this drive can have positive results in terms of increased productivity and greater financial reward. Many successful entrepreneurs and hard-driving business executives are propelled—sometimes unknowingly—by the fear of failure.

The danger, however, is that money and possessions become our primary measures of success and significance. Anything that threatens our ability to accumulate wealth becomes a driving force in our decision-making processes. Ultimately this mind-set leads to unwise decisions and wrong financial moves.

Once I recognized how common—and powerful—the fear of failure was, I began to recognize its presence in my decision making. When I launched my financial advisory firm, I was determined not to allow my own fear and my own need for significance to establish a foothold. I refused to continue my workaholic lifestyle. I tried to set an example that let my employees know they were not expected to work long hours at night or on weekends.

I faced the fear of failure, not only on a financial level, but also on a spiritual level. If you're a Christian, you have already dealt with this issue. You are already an admitted failure! You have recognized that you can do nothing to save yourself or to earn your own significance.

Jesus Christ is the only true source of personal worth and fulfillment. As 2 Corinthians 3:5 reminds us, we are not "sufficient," or competent, to claim anything for ourselves, "but our sufficiency is from God" (NKJV). Once we truly believe this promise, the fear of failure—and its accompanying desires for material or worldly significance—will no longer dictate our decisions and behavior.

Another common fear to identify is the fear of the future. My mother was a very gifted worrier. She seemed to feel that if she worried enough she could somehow manipulate the future. Worry is simply a misguided attempt to control future events. Most of what we worry about never comes to pass (causing the worrying skeptic to respond that worry indeed works!).

The things we worry about—such as the death of a spouse, a medical emergency, unrealized dreams, or a financial calamity—are the things that affect our peace of mind. Again, identifying this fear is half the battle. Once we recognize that we're afraid of the future, we can pinpoint the exact problem and then either develop an effective solution or recognize the outcome is out of our control. As with the fear of failure, we must evaluate the fear of the future on two levels, the spiritual and the financial.

Scripture is loaded with truth and wisdom about the future and how we are to approach it. In Luke 14:28 Jesus asks, "Which of you, intending to build a tower, does not sit down first and count the cost, whether he has enough to finish it?" (NKJV). Obviously, there is wisdom in accurate financial planning for the future.

At the same time, though, the Bible warns us that we cannot control the future. James 4:14 reminds us that we "do not know what will happen tomorrow. For what is your life? It is even a vapor that appears for a little time and then vanishes away" (NKJV).

One of my favorite passages about the future and the time we have is 2 Peter 3:8: "With the Lord one day is as a thousand years, and a thousand years as one day" (NKJV).

Joni Eareckson Tada once told me her thoughts on this verse. Paralyzed after a diving accident, Joni is a popular author, speaker, and artist who has a dynamic ministry to the disabled. I had always interpreted 2 Peter 3:8 to mean that since a day is like a thousand years, God is not anxious about schedules or timetables. After all, He has all the time in the world! While I still believe this assessment to be true, Joni opened my eyes to the other side of this verse. Since a thousand years is like a day, Joni said, each day becomes incredibly important in that it can have the eternal impact of a thousand years!

The spiritual principles outlined in 2 Peter 3:8 are also appropriate on a financial level. The knowledge that time is not as short as it may appear to be will keep us from plunging headlong into an ill-considered plan or investment. On the other hand, the realization of each day's potential can motivate us to action where we might otherwise drag our feet. Either way, the smartest approach to any financial decision begins with confronting our concerns.

Related to our fear of the future is our fear that we might miss out on an opportunity. Surefire "opportunities of a lifetime" arise every day, from business deals to stock market finds. These opportunities should be viewed with a skeptical eye, keeping in mind three observations: First, if it sounds too good to be true, it probably is. Second, you never hear about "bad" deals. No one pitches a bad deal; they're all promoted as good deals. Finally, you won't miss the opportunity of a lifetime because there's always another guaranteed opportunity coming tomorrow.

## How Fear Can Sabotage Your Financial Decisions

We've known of people who feared the economy or government was collapsing. So they sold investments, stocked food, and started withdrawing from society. How can you tell if a decision is motivated by fear or simply by conservative caution? A gloom-and-doom forecast may lead to some reasonable predictions, but it shouldn't be the foundation of your decision making.

Fear-based decisions may be characterized by one or more of the following traits:

- The decision is made quickly, with little forethought.
- The decision is presumptive, based on conclusions that have little or no substantiating proof.
- The decision is ill-advised, having been made under the counsel of untested, unreliable, or biased sources.

A fear-based decision is often accompanied by a gut reaction of anxiety and tension. By contrast, wise and thoughtful decisions are accompanied by a sense of stability and calm. The Bible attests to this pattern. Philippians 4:7 promises that "the peace of God, which transcends all understanding, will guard your hearts and your minds in Christ Jesus." Good decisions, financial and otherwise, are marked by peace, not panic.

Fear can ruin even the best-laid financial plans. Equally devastating, though, is the inability to act. Fear of making a wrong decision can result in our making no decision at all. We may get caught in "analysis paralysis," endlessly weighing our options until we are completely unable to make a move of any kind.

As you consider any financial decision, three simple questions are useful in gauging your degree of panic, paralysis, or peace:

1. What is the very worst that can happen if I do (or do not do) this?
2. How likely is that worst-case scenario?
3. Am I willing to live with the consequences—favorable or not—of this decision?

The answers to these questions will help remove the biases created by fear and greed, allow you to view your options objectively, and help you honestly evaluate your level of peace.

Probably the greatest temptation during times of economic uncertainty is to hoard your wealth. Fear and uncertainty can create the following three temptations:

- A longing for a life of comfort and ease.
- The perceived right to a particular lifestyle.
- The desire to be protected from any consequences of economic uncertainty.

Because you've carried, petted, and nurtured your fears, they can worm their way back into your financial life and create panic. Don't let them paralyze you and keep you from acting. When you feel fears returning, be sure to review the questions and strategies in this chapter. Let's move on to the steps you can proactively take to protect your personal finances in uncertain times.

## CHAPTER 4

# THIS ISN'T GOING TO HURT A BIT. . . .

## Step 1: Take a Financial Physical

Joseph is one of our heroes. After being sold into slavery by his jealous brothers, he was sexually propositioned and then slandered by his boss's wife. As a result, he was thrown into prison, where he was forgotten for years. Despite his circumstances, Joseph remained faithful to God. Even the lure of sudden fame and prosperity failed to tempt him to turn away from the Lord.

Our spirits are attracted to Joseph's faithfulness. Our minds, though, are impressed by something else. As financial advisors and accountants, we find Joseph's ability to handle resources and prepare a strategy for the future particularly appealing. He had no academic or vocational training. Even so, thanks to his foresight and effective planning, he was able to thrive during a worldwide economic catastrophe.

Joseph's story, detailed in Genesis 39–41, offers valuable lessons for us today. We're told Joseph was "handsome in form and appearance" (39:6, NKJV). When he resisted the sexual advances of his master's wife, she had him thrown into prison on trumped-up charges of attempted rape.

During his imprisonment, Joseph developed a reputation as an interpreter of dreams. When this talent came to Pharaoh's attention, he called on Joseph to explain two disturbing dreams.

After listening to Pharaoh's account of the visions, Joseph revealed their meaning: Egypt was destined for seven years of agricultural abundance followed by seven years of severe famine. That was the economic forecast.

Joseph then recommended a plan for storing food during the good years so the nation could survive the lean. Pharaoh liked the suggestion. He liked Joseph's confidence and immediately placed the young Hebrew as chief operating officer to run all of Egypt.

## A Proactive Plan: Lessons from Joseph

Joseph began his tenure as Egypt's COO by touring the country to assess the state of the nation. At the time the harvests were plentiful. We imagine Joseph surveyed the territory, noted population levels and needs, monitored crops and grain production, and considered storage alternatives.

Next, he established a goal. Simply put, Joseph wanted Egypt to survive the seven years of famine that lay ahead.

Finally, Joseph developed a plan. During the seven years

---

### 8 THINGS NOT TO SKIMP ON DURING TOUGH ECONOMIC TIMES

1. Giving (acknowledging God's provision in this way really does bring peace)

2. Mortgage payment and property taxes

3. Utilities

4. Car maintenance

5. Health insurance

6. Fun times with your spouse and kids (just look for the many free or low-cost options available)

7. Patience and long-term vision

8. Bible reading and prayer

---

of abundance that preceded the famine, he "gathered very much grain, as the sand of the sea, until he stopped counting, for it was immeasurable" (Genesis 41:49, NKJV).

Joseph's approach parallels the strategy you can employ for your own financial future. Like Joseph, use a three-pronged attack:

1. **Take a financial physical.** The beginning point of responsible, proactive money management is to determine the actual state of your finances. Most people are simply not realistic about where they are financially. If a person's physical health were at stake, he or she would certainly be candid with a physician. Just as a doctor needs the proper facts to make a correct diagnosis, a financial physical must also be completely accurate and honest.

2. **Establish a finish line.** Decide where you want to go, and then develop sound financial goals. Whether you want to provide for a college education, debt reduction, retirement, a down payment on a house, long-term giving, or something else, you must establish the objectives, discuss them openly with your spouse if you are married, write them down, and keep them in prayer.

3. **Plan how to get from here to there.** An effective strategy to move from point one to point two is implementing the four principles of financial success:

   > Think long term with your goals and investing.
   > Learn to live within your income.
   > Become your own bank (increase your liquidity).
   > Get out of debt.

## The Critical Questions for a Financial Physical

A financial physical involves answering four significant questions:

1. What do I owe?
2. What do I own?

3. How much am I spending?
4. How strong are my safety nets?

There are no wrong answers to these questions. Couples should be able to work jointly on their assessment without fear of criticism, condemnation, or conflict.

**What do I owe?** Most Americans have more debts than they do assets. Sadly, this is due not so much to big-ticket items such as a home mortgage as it is to a hefty load of smaller things like installment and credit card debt. Over time, a person's financial balance sheet only gets more lopsided as these debt-financed purchases decrease in value.

The good news is that consumers finally seem to be growing more aware of their precarious situation. Today's "debt generation" is waking up to the danger of its individual deficits at last.

You saw the danger of leverage (taking on additional debt and risk in hopes of greater profits) in banking and financial institutions during the credit crisis of 2008. Yet individual consumers have often been cavalier about their own revolving credit. For years, they could simply move one credit card's balance to a new account, issued by a lender offering zero percent interest on transfer balances. Such offers are becoming much rarer, just as credit card issuers are jacking up interest rates when cardholders miss their payments.

Years ago the late Lewis Grizzard wrote a newspaper column illustrating an extremely nonchalant attitude toward debt. He told the story about a former coworker who received a letter from one of his creditors:

"They're mad about the fact that I missed a payment," he said.

"The way I pay my bills is I put them all in a hat. Then I reach into the hat without looking and pull out a bill.

"I keep doing that until I'm out of money. There are always a few bills left in the hat, but at least everybody I owe has the same chance of being pulled out of the hat.

"I wrote the people back and told them if they sent me another nasty letter I wouldn't even put them in the hat anymore."[11]

As painful as it may seem at first, we need to confront our indebtedness. No financial physical is complete without an honest picture of the liabilities column. Even if your situation seems overwhelming, this step cannot be overlooked. By openly admitting how much you owe, you can take a hopeful—rather than hopeless—approach to the future.

We recommend you make two lists, one for credit card only; the other for all other debts. Tally what you owe, compiling the following information for each debt in a spreadsheet or on paper:

- **Creditor:** who you owe
- **Initial amount borrowed:** the amount borrowed at the beginning of the loan
- **Current balance due:** the amount of money you initially borrowed plus any accrued interest or finance changes less any payments you have made against the loan
- **Minimum monthly payments:** the smallest monthly payment your creditor will allow without causing your account to be considered delinquent

**What do I own?** Most people don't really know what they own. It's a good idea, even if only for insurance purposes, to have a well-documented listing of your possessions.[12] You can preserve this on paper, in photographs, on DVD, or in a computer listing.

Completing the inventory is not as difficult as it may seem; items such as silverware, jewelry, or clothing may be categorized simply as "household goods." Determine the worth of your assets based on their fair market value—the amount an objective, independent person would pay for this asset.

Once you have determined the sum total of your assets, subtract your debts to figure your net worth. Should your net worth turn out to be a negative number, take heart: Most Americans are in the same position! This, however, is where you don't want to be normal. With competent money management, your net worth can grow—even in times of economic uncertainty.

**How much am I spending?** Once you have determined your net worth, you need to get a handle on how fast that amount is growing or shrinking. To do this, you must track your spending patterns to see where—and how fast—the money goes.

One couple got into an argument over the wife's spending habits. Her assessment of the situation differed markedly from her husband's. "The problem is not my overspending," she told him. "It's your under-depositing!"

Men and women fall into the same spending trap. More often than not, the problem is fueled by unexpected impulse purchases. By monitoring our actual spending patterns, we discover how much of the outflow is going toward regular, predictable expenses, such as housing and utilities, and how much is spent on spur-of-the moment "must-have" purchases, such as the latest cell phone or electronic device.

Chapter 6 offers more details for spending smart. For now, though, you can get a big-picture perspective on your purchasing habits by saving receipts and credit card statements. Go through your checkbook register. Keep track of all of your expenses over

---

**7 QUESTIONS TO ASK BEFORE YOU MAKE A PURCHASE**

1. Do I really need this?

2. Can I borrow it, rent it, or try it before purchasing it?

3. Will I change my mind because of cost once I have it?

4. What will I have to cut back on to buy this?

5. Have I had a cooling-off period to avoid making an impulse purchase?

6. Have I checked with my spouse or accountability friend?

7. Have I compared prices on the Internet or other sources?

a one- to three-month period. The information you glean may surprise you. It may prove useful for pinpointing patterns and correcting any problems you discover.

**How strong are my safety nets?** Your safety nets protect you and help you withstand a catastrophe. Life and disability insurance, health care coverage, and property and casualty policies are essential parts of your total safety package.

In a recent survey related to safety nets, 86 percent said that people should have life insurance. Yet with a do-what-I-say, not-what-I-do approach, 25 percent of those who said people should have life insurance didn't have it for themselves.[13]

Our book *Faith-Based Family Finances* contains a detailed worksheet you can use to assess your life insurance needs. You might also wish to check with a reputable financial advisor to see if your safety nets have any holes. Plan to review all of your insurance coverage periodically as your family size and needs change. Your policies' limits may be too high or too low.

## Somebody's Watching You

All four of the steps we have covered—determining how much you owe, how much you own, how much you spend, and how well you are protected—are essential to a thorough and complete financial physical. Once you have an accurate picture of your situation, you can set goals and plan to achieve them.

Like Joseph, you must travel throughout your entire "land" to get a well-defined picture of your situation. If you begin at the beginning and take care to set goals and follow a wise and proper strategy, you will reap the benefits of successful stewardship.

You won't be the only one who benefits from this process. The famine in Joseph's day extended throughout the world. Nowhere could any food be found except in Egypt. Joseph threw open the storehouses, selling grain to Egyptians and foreigners alike. The entire world descended on Egypt, turning to Joseph and his abundant provisions to meet their desperate need.

Through it all, Joseph never forgot the Lord. He credited God with bringing him to Egypt, making him a ruler over the land, and saving lives during the terrible famine.

Like Joseph, we also have the opportunity to direct the world's eyes toward the Lord. As we prosper during times of economic uncertainty, people will be drawn to us for answers. Our proactive approach, demonstrated through wise financial stewardship, will attract attention. As Jesus instructed us in Matthew 5:16, we can "let [our] light shine before men, that they may see [our] good deeds and praise [our] Father in heaven."

The world is watching. Will you be like Joseph? In the next chapter you will learn how to develop your own financial strategy by setting goals and planning how to achieve them. As you do, remember that God can give you the perspective and the wisdom to face an economically uncertain future.

## CHAPTER 5

# AIM AT NOTHING AND YOU'LL HIT IT EVERY TIME

## Step 2: Think Long Term—Set Goals

We know what you're thinking after seeing this chapter subtitle: *Oh, come on, do I have to? Do I really need to bother with writing down goals?*

We have taught and written about the importance of goal setting for many years. Many people just want to skip this step and go to implementing action steps. But don't pass Go. Don't collect your $200 yet.

As we've worked with people through the years, we've observed a direct relationship between goal setting and accomplishment. We were pleased to find out about a study backing up our personal observations. The subjects of the study were Harvard students working toward their master of business administration (MBA) degrees. At the 10-year reunion of a specific graduating class, researchers found that about 3 percent of these Harvard MBAs had accomplished far more than the other 97 percent. In fact, they were earning, on average, 10 times as much as the other 97 percent put together! What made the difference? The primary distinguishing characteristic was that the 3 percent had left Harvard as twentysomethings with written goals.[14]

Taking the financial physical provides you with the information you need to begin setting goals. The very prospect of undergoing a physical, for example, can motivate you to improve your financial health. Likewise, the mere act of defining a goal puts you that much closer to achieving it.

Both of us remember going through extensive health physicals at key ages in our lives. Sheer vanity compelled us to begin getting in shape even before any tests were performed. After the physicals, we easily identified several very logical goals: eating right, getting proper exercise, and scheduling periodic checkups. They quickly became part of our regular routine. Other goals required more thought and planning. The point is that setting goals—and planning how to achieve them—came as a natural outgrowth of the physical evaluation process.

In the last chapter you took your financial physical. Based on that assessment, you can now set goals that will provide direction, motivation, and discipline in your financial life. These benefits make goal setting an integral part of any endeavor. In times of economic uncertainty, however, carefully considered and well-defined goals take on added significance. Goals and dreams that are taken for granted during periods of prosperity may require a new strategy or additional effort when times are tough.

Bill Behre and his family represent the "dawning Age of Frugality," according to *Business Week*. Even though Behre has a stable job as a dean at the College of New Jersey, he and his family realized their lavish spending could cause problems down the road. Now they walk everywhere, sometimes buy clothing at consignment shops, and eat out very rarely.

"After 9/11 it became patriotic to shop," Behre says, "and we became as patriotic as anybody." In fact they took out a $101,000 home equity loan on a previous house, which helped pay for several cruises and annual family vacations to Disney World. However, as they took stock of their own financial condition, they realized that their overconsumption could lead to serious problems.[15] They wanted financial independence and determined the steps they needed to take to eliminate their debt.

Review the results of your own financial physical. As you weigh your position, ask yourself some difficult questions:

- Do I need to accelerate debt repayment?
- Is my mortgage payment (plus insurance and taxes for my house) more than 30 percent of my income?
- Am I financially flexible enough to handle the loss of a job or the loss of an investment?
- Does my spending reflect concern over economic uncertainty—or am I presuming upon the future?
- Do I consistently make giving a top priority—or is it one of the first areas to go when finances are tight?
- How risk-proof are my investments? What do I depend on them for?
- Have I planned for future taxes? If I had to sell an investment, could I meet the tax obligations?

Questions like these help sharpen your perspective on your financial circumstances. They also serve as the foundation for the following five-step process that allows you to create a roster of clearly defined, target-oriented goals.

## Your "Bucket List" of Financial Goals

In the movie *The Bucket List*, two terminally ill cancer patients decide to go out in style. They compose a bucket list—things to do before they kick the bucket. On a crumpled yellow sheet of paper, they write down everything from sky diving to driving a race car around a track. You may not have a terminal disease, but what are your financial goals before you kick the bucket? Here are five steps to setting goals:

1. **List your goals.** Psalm 37:4 says, "Delight yourself in the LORD and he will give you the desires of your heart." If you trust Him to do so, God promises to put the right desires

in your heart. Working from this perspective, make a list of your financial dreams and goals. Perhaps you want to trim your spending and eliminate your credit card debt over the next year. You may wish to start your own business or retire in a place near your grandchildren. Maybe you have two children to put through college. Perhaps you contribute to an overseas orphanage and want to save for a short-term mission trip there. What about those piano or tennis lessons the kids want? Have you figured out how to pay for them?

**Let your imagination wander.** As you reflect, ask God to help you establish objectives that will give your life purpose and direction. The suggested Financial Goal-Setting Topics at the conclusion of this chapter may help you think through your needs and desires. Having prayerfully considered your goals, make a list of everything you would like to achieve, from career hopes to vacation dreams to savings plans.

### My Goals and Dreams

DATE: _____

(For example, reduce debt) _____

(For example, pay off credit cards)_____

_____

_____

_____

_____

_____

_____

_____

_____

_____

_____

2. **Consolidate and refine.** You have made your list; now check it twice. See if there are things that you have unintentionally jotted down more than once. Perhaps, as in the example

above, you listed "reduce debt" and "pay off credit cards." You may be able to blend these goals into just one objective. The idea is to refine your list so that it reflects a roster of clearly stated, distinct goals.

### Consolidated Goals and Dreams

DATE: _____

(For example, reduce debt by paying off the gas credit card)

_____

_____

_____

_____

_____

_____

_____

_____

_____

_____

3. **Prioritize.** Some of your goals will obviously be more important than others. Using your consolidated list, evaluate each goal and place it into one of the following categories (use another sheet of paper if you need more space):

   **a. Indispensable goals.** An example of a "must-do" goal includes providing for a sick child. Economically, and in some cases physically, the items in this category simply must be done.

   1. _____

   2. _____

   3. _____

   **b. Important goals.** These may include objectives such as buying a home, providing for retirement, or sending a child to college. The things on this list will be high priorities, yet they are not absolutely vital to your survival.

1. _____
2. _____
3. _____

**c. Likes and wants.** This category is for your desires. Perhaps you are eager to increase your giving percentage, or maybe you want to save for a family vacation. Those kinds of goals fit here.

1. _____
2. _____
3. _____

**d. Future dreams.** This list is your chance to think big. Do you hope to own your own business someday? Is your heart's desire to go into full-time Christian work—even if it means saying good-bye to your salary? Have you always wanted to take an extended tour through Europe? Economic uncertainty may make dreams like these seem remote, but do not discard them—particularly if your dream is one you feel God has put on your heart.

1. _____
2. _____
3. _____

**e. Goals that others think you should have.** The final grouping on your list is for those things that other people think you need. You may not agree with the financial advisor who thinks you should increase your insurance coverage. You may not see the urgency your mother does when she begs you to settle down and buy a home. You may be unsure that buying the car your teenager wants is a wise move right now. Even so, if the goal seems even remotely logical or legitimate to you, write it down for consideration.

1. _____
2. _____
3. _____

Your individual circumstances will dictate how you group your objectives. Buying a new car may be important for the woman whose job depends on reliable transportation, while the purchase is only a "want" for the man who is just plain tired of driving his ugly old clunker.

Once you have listed and categorized your goals, pick your top five priorities. Your list may include a dozen or five dozen objectives; you probably can't pursue all or even most of them. Narrow your choices to the five most pressing concerns.

This selection process forces you to examine your priorities. Your decisions may be marked by tension, especially as you juggle short- and long-term goals.

Suppose, for example, that your resources are limited. You want to save a substantial amount to send your child to college. You're also dying to get away for a much-needed weekend alone with your spouse. Both goals are legitimate. One is a long-term objective. The other is a short-term desire, yet the health of your marriage today will have long-term consequences. It's up to you to weigh the options. Sacrificing something is usually required.

### Top Five Goals

DATE: _____

1. _____
2. _____
3. _____
4. _____
5. _____

4. **Quantify your five goals.** Once you have selected your top five priorities, define them in numeric terms—how much money and/or time will be required to reach your objective. If you can't quantify a goal, you can't pursue it effectively.

I (Jeremy) wanted to improve my tennis rating before my

fortieth birthday. That goal established the time frame I had to work in. My wife, Sharon, and I began tithing early in our marriage and later set a goal to increase our charitable giving as a percentage of income by 0.5 percent each year. By attaching a numerical percentage to our desire to give, we could recognize and press toward the finish line. Be as specific as you can as you quantify and define your goals.

### Top Five Goals Quantified

DATE: _____

(Example: Save $75 per month for a family vacation next summer)

1. _____
2. _____
3. _____
4. _____
5. _____

5. **Keep your goals visible.** Your goals must be seen easily and often if you hope to stay on the right track. I (Ron) keep a notebook that includes all the goals that my wife, Judy, and I have ever written. Others post goals on car dashboards, by kitchen sinks, inside checkbook covers—anywhere they will be seen and remembered. Wallace Johnson, the highly successful cofounder of Holiday Inn, always kept a list of his top ten priorities on a three-by-five card attached to his bathroom mirror.

In addition to keeping your goals visible, you must also plan to take an even closer look at them from time to time. A periodic review is necessary to see which goals need to be revised or eliminated, where additions might need to be made, and which goals may be happily checked off the list and moved into the "accomplishments" category.

Goal setting is dynamic. We've heard Dr. Howard Hendricks say God is interested in getting us moving. He gets us moving through our goal setting. But we should write our goals in sand, not concrete. If we set a faith goal and begin to move toward it, God can intervene and change the goal in time and amount. Goal setting is a faith process; we make decisions by faith. Remember that "without faith it is impossible to please God" (Hebrews 11:6).

We'd suggest writing your goals along these lines:

I believe God would have me to _____.

How do you know what God would have you to do? Spend time talking with God about it. Then write down your impressions, make those impressions measurable, and take action. Setting goals is not a process of ignoring God and relying on self. You should focus on what God directs you to do.

After you set your faith financial goals, here are three overall checkup and accountability questions:

1. What does your spouse think about this goal?
2. What is the motive behind your goal—your glory or God's glory?
3. What would God think about your goal?

## Do You Want to Get Away? Have a Goal-Setting Retreat

Perhaps the thought of setting goals—financial or otherwise—seems overwhelming with all the demands on your time. If so, consider the approach I (Ron) and my wife took when our kids were at home. Once a year, we escaped our regular routine and five children for a weekend getaway. A little relaxation, a little romance, a little talking, a little planning—they all do wonders for a marriage relationship.

Besides working on communication and the family schedule, we set financial goals and reviewed the ones from previous years. Although I'm describing a scenario for married couples, a goal-setting time is just as important for single adults too. You may also want to look at physical, parenting, relational, and spiritual goals. But this is a financial book, so here's a list of financial topics to get you started:

## Financial Goal-Setting Topics
### Saving Goals
How much do we need?
How should we save? Weekly? Monthly? Annual bonus?
Why? What are we saving for?

### Debt Goals
How much is okay?
Should we avoid it altogether?
Should we get out of it?

### Lifestyle Goals
What kind of house do we need or want?
Do we want to take a vacation? Where?
What about areas like autos, entertainment, clothing, etc.?

### Education Goals for Children or Self
Public or private schooling?
College? University?
Trade school?

### Vacation Goals
How many this year?
Where to go?
With kids? Without?

### Insurance Goals
Life, home, health, auto, other
How much do we need?
What kind of policy suits our needs?

### Giving Goals
How much to give?
Where to give?
When to give? Weekly? Biweekly? Monthly?

**Tax Goals**

Do we reduce our taxes?
How can we manage them?
Do we underwithhold?
Do we overwithhold?

**Career Goals**

Starting a business?
Advancement?
Job satisfaction? Location?

**Household Goals**

When, where, and what kind of home to buy/rent?
Furniture needed?
Special needs: replace appliance, add room for guests
or home office, etc.?

**Investment Goals**

Where to invest?
Why invest?
How much to invest?

## CHAPTER 6

# I'M STUCK IN A TRAFFIC JAM ON THE ROAD TO RICHES

### Step 3: Spend Less Than You Earn

It doesn't matter how much you make. It doesn't matter whether your idea of a big treat is to buy tickets to the movies or tickets for a cruise. No matter how much money you have, no matter how much more you can earn, there will always be unlimited ways to allocate limited resources.

Choices have to be made. Tough choices. This is especially true for Americans living in a culture and economy with unlimited options to spend money at the mall, at Stuff-Mart, or on the Internet. Advertisers and easily accessible credit further stoke our desires, making purchasing decisions even more difficult.

People often want to appear like they're doing well financially. So they buy into the advertising appeal of expensive goods, luxury items, and designer labels. In the interesting book *The Millionaire Next Door*, professors Thomas Stanley and William Danko point out that self-made millionaires operate very differently:

- They live below their means, drive cars older than three years old, wear inexpensive suits, and know what they spend on household items.[16]
- Fifty-five percent of millionaires operate on an annual

budget. Most who don't budget say they follow a strict "pay yourself before spending it strategy" and set aside at least 15 percent of their income before spending it.[17]

- Contrary to the image we have of celebrities, athletes, and the rich and famous living lavishly, the large majority of millionaires buy inexpensive watches, avoid luxury cars, shun car leases, and don't own mansions but opt for mortgage-free homes in nice neighborhoods.[18]

After years of studying and researching the typical millionaire, the authors stated, "What are three words that profile the affluent? Frugal, frugal, frugal. Being frugal is the cornerstone of wealth building."[19]

We've known and taught this for years, but it's affirming to have PhDs and thousands of millionaires confirm it. Spend less than you earn, and you will do well financially over time. The ancient wisdom of Solomon, probably the world's first billionaire, echoed the same idea: "He who gathers money little by little makes it grow" (Proverbs 13:11).

We don't know anyone who intentionally sets out to spend more than they make every month. Nobody sets a New Year's resolution to spend 15 percent more than they earn. Our yearnings exceed our earnings. Unanticipated expenses come. Things break. Prices rise. Emergencies happen. Life just seems to spin out of control.

It doesn't matter what you make. It does matter that you have something left over. Even the sharpest Wall Street whiz can't make money for you if you spend it all. Even the strongest marriages can begin to buckle under the pressure of consistently spending more than the couple earns.

## How to Keep from Spending Again What Is Already Spent

Controlling spending sounds like a lot of work. Most other Americans don't do it. It's easier to put the surprises on the credit cards. What's in it for you? Here are the rewards of smart spending:

- Spending less than you earn decreases the likelihood of debt.
- Spending less than you earn makes saving money possible.
- Spending less than you earn decreases the possibility of future financial problems.

Does it sound like we're about to bring up the B word: *budget*? Call it a strategic spending plan if you don't like the B word. If you don't think you need a strategic spending plan, take a moment to answer a few diagnostic questions:

- Have you and your spouse ever argued over financial matters?
- Have you ever impulsively bought a car or major appliance?
- Do you routinely fail to balance your checkbook?
- Do you bounce checks more than once a year, or do you frequently rely on an overdraft protection credit line?
- Have you ever tried using a budget, but given up after only a few weeks or months?
- Do you occasionally or frequently receive past due notices?
- Do you use credit cards for car repairs or other emergency expenses?
- Are your credit cards at or near their limit?
- Do you use credit cards to meet your living expenses (groceries, eating out, etc.)?
- Do you routinely pay only the minimum amount due on credit accounts?
- Have you ever considered or received a consolidation loan?
- Do you frequently dip into savings to meet expenses?
- Do you have less than three months' worth of living expenses in cash available in savings or money market funds?

- Have you ever borrowed money from friends or relatives and failed to repay the loan according to the agreed terms?
- Do you worry or lose sleep over the level of your mortgage?
- Have you had any bills turned over to a collection agency?

If you answered yes to more than three of these questions, your future financial security may be at risk. A smart spending plan can help safeguard your finances. We're not saying you have to start hoarding your pennies or cut out all the fun. Instead we want to encourage you to develop a plan for effective spending—one that allows you to allocate your resources among the best possible alternatives to help you meet your short- and long-term goals. The sooner you start planning, the better.

---

**4 INNOVATIVE WAYS TO GIVE DURING AN ECONOMIC DOWNTURN**

1. Give time.

2. Give appreciated stock.

3. Donate useful used items.

4. Donate special skills.

---

## Let's Simplify: There Are Only Five Uses of Money

As we mentioned, there are unlimited options for spending your money. That's overwhelming. But if we group all those options, there are really only five uses of money in the short term. Let's simplify these options to help you focus better:

> Giving
> Taxes
> Saving/investing
> Short-term debt repayment
> Lifestyle choices

# SHORT-TERM USES OF MONEY
### 5 Buckets to be filled

In the short term, every spending decision fits into one of these five uses, or categories. How much of your money should go into each category? We can't give you exact amounts. The Bible doesn't command us to dedicate a certain percentage to each area—although it gives us many principles and guidelines about each one of these five areas. You'll need to study these and then decide, with your family and financial advisor, if you have one, what you'll allocate to each.

The most challenging bucket to control is lifestyle. Certainly, you are expected to provide for your family's needs. You may be surprised at how strongly the Bible states this point: "If anyone does not provide for his own, and especially for those of his household, he has denied the faith and is worse than an unbeliever" (1 Timothy 5:8, NKJV).

You probably are able to meet all your needs, though perhaps not all your wants and desires. Lifestyle becomes the top priority of most people, with giving falling to fourth or fifth priority. Their reasoning often goes like this: "I'd like to give, but by the time I pay my taxes, repay my debts, and provide for my family, there's just not enough left over to give." Yet even in difficult economic times, the giving bucket needs to filled. Giving is strong evidence of living a life of faith rather than living in fear with a focus on present circumstances.

Though there isn't room in this book to focus on the mechanics of budgeting, see www.masteryourmoney.com, *Faith-Based Family Finances,* and our book *The New Master Your Money* for more detailed worksheets that will enable you to set up your spending plan. The CliffsNotes version of controlling your lifestyle spending reads like this:

1. Estimate your living expenses.
2. Record your actual spending.
3. Refine your spending plan.
4. Control your spending plan.
5. Evaluate and revise, revise, revise.

## Keep Simplifying: Look at the Six Common Long-Term Goals

You've seen the five uses of money in the short term. Once you have spent money on the other four areas, you hope there's some flow into the Investment/Savings bucket. Actually, you shouldn't just hope; you should plan for it. When there is a surplus, or margin, your net worth grows. As your net worth grows, you can use the accumulated assets to meet your long-term goals. While everyone's goals are somewhat unique, most long-term goals tend to fall under one of the following categories:

- Retirement
- Family needs
- Maximized giving
- Lifestyle desires
- Debt elimination
- Business start-up

# LONG-TERM GOALS
### 6 MORE Buckets to be filled

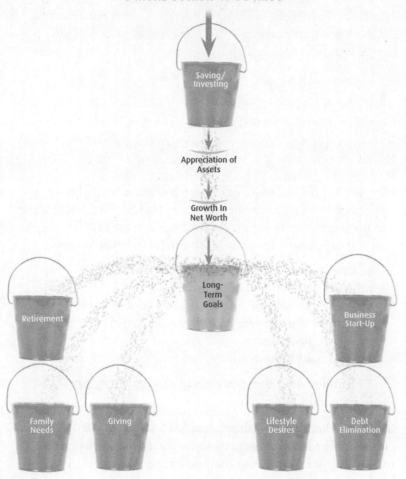

## Integrating Your Short- and Long-Term Planning

As you consider the five short-term uses and six long-term uses of income, the "Biblical Financial Decision Making" diagram on page 63 will help you put it all together. This diagram shows your

## 7 QUESTIONS TO CONSIDER AS YOU CREATE YOUR SPENDING PLAN

1. What is my spendable income?

2. What have I been spending over the last 12 to 24 months?

3. What are my current debt obligations?

4. What would I like to spend?

5. In what ways would my future be improved if I spent less?

6. What expenses are fixed and out of my control?

7. What expenses do I have control over?

income in a bucket. Money flows out like water from a bucket as you pour much of it into the short-term buckets. You should strive to have some money left to fill your long-term buckets. This begins an ongoing process. Here's an outline of this five-step process:

Step 1: Summarize your present situation.
Step 2: Establish your financial goals.
Step 3: Decide the priority of each bucket.
Step 4: Manage your cash flow according to those priorities.
Step 5: Monitor results.

This financial decision-making diagram illustrates three very important implications:

- There are no independent financial decisions.
- The longer term perspective you have, the better the possibility of your making a good financial decision now.
- Financial decisions have lifetime implications.

## Spending Less Is Better Than Making More

When most people consider improving their cash flow, they think of ways they could increase their income. They consider

# BIBLICAL FINANCIAL DECISION MAKING

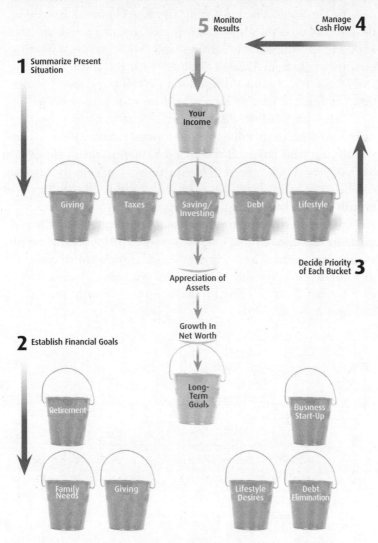

**5** Monitor Results

Manage Cash Flow **4**

**1** Summarize Present Situation

Your Income

Giving  Taxes  Saving/ Investing  Debt  Lifestyle

Decide Priority of Each Bucket **3**

Appreciation of Assets

Growth In Net Worth

**2** Establish Financial Goals

Retirement

Long-Term Goals

Business Start-Up

Family Needs  Giving  Lifestyle Desires  Debt Elimination

working extra hours, taking on another job, starting a side business, or moving to a better-paying job. Keep in mind, however, the effect of taxes on additional income. To end up with an extra $100 net effect upon your family's cash flow, you would have to earn anywhere from $120 to $150 before taxes. Social Security and Medicare tax withholdings, local payroll taxes, state income taxes, and federal income taxes all reduce your take-home pay.

You want to know a more effective way to improve your cash flow? Reduce spending, which provides a more tax-efficient way to help your family. If you spend $100 less, then your family has $100 more. Compared to having to work to earn money that will be taxed before it reaches your wallet, reducing spending sounds like the easier way to make money.

Whether you're currently enjoying good economic times or suffering through difficult ones, you may need specific help with money-saving ideas. In the appendix, we've included an assortment of 40 money-saving ideas to help your family's cash flow even further. Start reducing expenses right away with these ideas and explanations.

## CHAPTER 7

# I'M HAVING AN OUT-OF-MONEY EXPERIENCE

### Step 4: Build Emergency Savings

"Good news, Dad," began my (Ron's) daughter, Denise, recently. "Mark received a promotion. We'll be moving soon from Tampa to Denver."

After the initial few days of excitement for my son-in-law's career advancement, the reality of the decline in the real estate market set in. Florida real estate had appreciated significantly during much of the 2000s, but houses were not selling now—even at reduced prices.

Housing prices had declined in Denver, too, but not as much as in Tampa. Denise and Mark found a smaller house in Denver than the one they sold in Florida. Denise called me in the midst of the transition to Denver. Rather upset, she shared, "Dad, we lost all our equity in our Florida house."

I consoled her and agreed how difficult that is. I then added, "Well, at least you had equity to lose."

"But that's not all," she moaned. "We used up our emergency savings for the down payment on the Denver house."

"Well, honey," I responded, "as bad as that is, at least you had an emergency fund."

My daughter was disappointed in the setback of their balance sheet (what they own and owe). But the good news is that their monthly expenses didn't really change. Mark and Denise certainly expect the promotion and transfer to be a positive financial move over the next few years with increased earnings. To take advantage of this opportunity, they needed emergency savings. If they had had no equity in their home and no savings, they might not have been able to make the move.

## Liquidity Does Not Imply You're All Wet

Having money available and accessible is important during the surprises of life. Financial nerds call this liquidity. Liquidity is simply the ease and speed with which an asset can be turned into cash.

Think of liquidity as available savings. It includes cash, bank accounts, or other holdings that can be converted to cash quickly. Certificates of deposit and savings bonds are other examples of liquid assets. Real estate lots or rental properties are not liquid assets.

Why is liquidity so important? It's simply because the future is so uncertain—companies downsize, cars break down, medical emergencies occur, and so on. A recent survey shows that one in ten Americans fears losing his or her job. Nearly 55 percent of Americans worry that they wouldn't be able to pay their medical costs if they had a serious injury.[20] Without liquid assets, such misfortunes can be catastrophic.

Liquidity—or having readily available cash (such as an emergency fund)—is a key aspect of financial flexibility. Large companies need liquidity. One reason some large financial institutions in the United States failed in 2008 was because of their liquidity problems. For individuals, liquidity often means the difference between going into debt and remaining debt free when unexpected events or expenses come up.

One reason families without liquid assets feel so much pressure is that our system is structured in such a way that the less money you have, the more things cost. The more money you have available, the less things cost. For example, if you have cash to buy consumer items like clothes and furniture, you do not need to use a credit card that will charge interest of 20 percent or more—not to mention other charges, such as late fees or annual fees just to carry the card.

Having cash gives you the choice of how you'll pay, where you'll buy, and when you'll pay. If you can pay your car insurance or term life insurance annually or semiannually, you'll pay less than if you pay monthly, without incurring interest costs.

Also, if you need to borrow money for items such as cars or furniture, you not only pay interest, but you are likely to have points, bank fees, loan insurance, and late-payment penalties. The same is true when you purchase a home. In addition to the debt cost, you have such expenses as credit report fees and settlement charges. These can amount to thousands of dollars. You'll also be hit with extra fees if you are late on a utility payment. You may even suffer the loss of service.

## How Much Emergency Savings Should I Maintain?

When you have cash available, you can take advantage of sales and often even negotiate lower prices. After determining the cost for my (Jeremy's) daughter's treatment, her orthodontist asked us to select one of two payment plans: monthly payments spread out over a couple of years or one cash payment up front—which was several hundred dollars less than the amount we'd have to pay if we chose monthly payments. Fortunately we had the money available to pay the entire amount at the start of her treatment.

So how much should you put in an emergency savings fund? Once again, there are no absolutes. It depends on your job security, level of living expenses, debt situation, plans for major purchases, and your own comfort level.

Three months' living expenses may be adequate for someone with job stability. If your job is susceptible to strikes and layoffs, saving four to six months of living expenses would be

**5 PLACES TO FIND EXTRA CASH TO
BUILD YOUR EMERGENCY FUND**

1. Consider using eBay or another online site to sell items you no longer use (garage sales also work, though they're likely to bring in less money).

2. Reduce income tax withholding if you regularly receive a large tax refund.

3. Save unexpected income, such as work bonuses and monetary gifts.

4. Combine or close small savings accounts.

5. Just as you make paying your monthly mortgage or utility bill a priority, so consider adding to your savings account a monthly obligation.

better. A person working on a 100 percent–commission basis may need six months' expenses (especially if the commissions come in random intervals).

A target starting point would be one month's living expenses in checking and two months' living expenses in savings.

## Investing for the Short Term

Remember that while the purpose of a long-term investment is to build one's assets, an emergency fund has a different purpose. It is used to provide liquidity. Your emergency fund should be kept in a place that offers at least a minimum amount of interest without any risk, such as a bank money market savings account or a money market fund. The intention is to have these funds readily available as cash without the risk of losing principal. Availability, not return, is the main goal.

Listed below are several options for parking your savings until needed. These options maintain a high degree of liquidity and safety, and they generate some investment return:

*1. Passbook savings accounts.* These savings accounts, offered through any bank or savings and loan, offer low interest rates. Consumers may qualify for higher rates if their account reaches a certain balance.

2. *Checking accounts.* Many banks offer interest-paying checking accounts at passbook savings rates (NOW accounts), if a minimum balance is maintained. In some cases, free checks may also be included. If you keep one month's living expenses in checking, you will probably qualify for these interest-bearing accounts. Beware: some banks have monthly service charges.

3. *Money market funds (also called money market mutual funds or daily money funds).* Most mutual fund companies, such as American Funds, Fidelity Investments, or Vanguard, offer these accounts. Money market funds usually pay higher rates of interest than the bank. The rates vary daily according to the prevailing market interest rates. The funds are as liquid as banks or credit unions. Most offer check-writing privileges. Although money market funds are not insured by the government through the Federal Deposit Insurance Corporation (FDIC) like bank deposits, they have not had significant defaults or losses historically. Money market funds are convenient parking places for short-term funds or funds being accumulated for investment. They offer liquidity, flexibility, and check writing all rolled into one package.

4. *Money market accounts.* These savings accounts offered by local banks pay interest at money market rates. They may require a minimum balance (e.g., $1,000) and limit you to writing three checks against your account each month. These accounts are insured by the FDIC.

5. *Credit unions.* Credit unions usually offer slightly higher interest rates than banks on both checking and savings accounts.

6. *Certificates of deposit (CD).* CDs can be a good place to park money as long as you don't need the money immediately. Banks and credit unions offer CDs with maturity dates that may vary from 90 days to six months to five years. If an emergency arises, you can either make a premature withdrawal or borrow from the bank using the CD as collateral. In this case, you are risking the probability of an emergency occurring before your CD matures against the increased yield you can get from this account. CDs charge a surrender penalty—usually six months of interest—for an early withdrawal.

## In Case of an Emergency . . .

An emergency fund enables you to deal with the financial consequences of life's uncertainties, such as repairs, medical expenses, job layoffs, and so on. After the crisis passes, you should try to replenish the emergency savings fund over the next several months.

Unfortunately some people dip into their emergency savings to pay for other wants and desires—not emergencies. After not using these savings for six months or more, it can be tempting to tap into them to fund gifts, impulse purchases, and vacations. Don't fall into this trap. Such discretionary purchases should be planned for in your family's spending plan.

Occasionally I meet someone who suggests that building an emergency savings fund indicates a lack of faith. If that's your perspective, consider Proverbs 6:6-8:

> *Go to the ant, you sluggard;*
> *consider its ways and be wise!*
> *It has no commander,*
> *no overseer or ruler,*
> *yet it stores its provisions in summer*
> *and gathers its food at harvest.*

The key to prudent savings is following a plan. Ask yourself, for example, what you are saving for and how much is needed. If cash is being accumulated simply because it gives you a good feeling or a sense of security, then you're probably following a hoarding plan rather than a savings plan. If your faith increases only as your bank account increases (or vice versa), then you don't have a money problem, you have a spiritual problem.

Yet creating an emergency savings fund is an important part of any balanced financial strategy. When parking money for emergency living expenses or short-term major purchases, look beyond the yield (which may sometimes be low) and determine how this sequential step can help you achieve your overall financial goals. Once you've established an emergency fund, you can start thinking about making bigger purchases.

## Following the Savings Steps in Sequence

Which should come first: Building emergency savings or reducing debt? Paying off credit cards or your mortgage? The "Investment Hierarchy" on page 72 outlines the sequence we recommend.

*Level 1: Eliminate all credit card and consumer debt.* This provides an immediate "investment return" of 12 percent to 21 percent. Not having to pay that interest cost each year is comparable to achieving the same rate of return on any monies invested by you. Therefore, it is the surest and highest form of investment return you can make.

*Level 2: Set aside three to six months' living expenses in an interest-bearing account.* This becomes the emergency fund and, in effect, your own bank. You may unexpectedly need money to cover a major purchase or major expense. You may see an opportunity to save by purchasing now instead of later. In any of these situations, you can borrow from yourself out of this account rather than from a lending institution. If you tap into this account for an emergency, replace it as soon as possible.

# INVESTMENT HIERARCHY

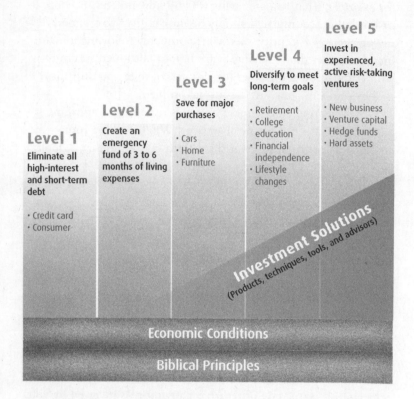

**Level 1**
Eliminate all high-interest and short-term debt

· Credit card
· Consumer

**Level 2**
Create an emergency fund of 3 to 6 months of living expenses

**Level 3**
Save for major purchases

· Cars
· Home
· Furniture

**Level 4**
Diversify to meet long-term goals

· Retirement
· College education
· Financial independence
· Lifestyle changes

**Level 5**
Invest in experienced, active risk-taking ventures

· New business
· Venture capital
· Hedge funds
· Hard assets

Investment Solutions
(Products, techniques, tools, and advisors)

Economic Conditions

Biblical Principles

Meeting these first two objectives is key to your personal financial growth and should be your priority before moving on to the next three levels. In other words, you do not go to level 5 until you've completed level 2. You should regularly ask yourself, *What's the best use of the next available dollar?* By doing so, you eliminate the need to make a decision whenever an investment alternative comes to you. If you have not already accomplished Level 1, then you let the "investment opportunity" go by. This takes discipline, but it's the right thing to do.

*Level 3: Save in an interest-bearing account for major purchases.*
These funds are allocated for the planned purchase of major
items such as automobiles, furniture, and even the down payment on a home.

*Level 4: Accumulate to meet long-term goals.* These might
include financial independence, college education, giving beyond the tithe, owning your own business, paying off
mortgage debt, and financing major lifestyle changes. All can be
funded through various investment alternatives. These investment alternatives provide a greater potential return to meet
your long-term goals and involve more risk, such as when you
invest in mutual funds through your employer's retirement plan.
However, you can likely accept more risk if you have a cash flow
margin, an emergency savings reserve, and little or no short-
term debt.

*Level 5: Invest in more experienced and active opportunities.* You
might choose to provide capital for a start-up business, buy raw
land for future subdivision developments, or buy bonds of a
distressed company in hopes of a turnaround. Use investment
dollars to speculate in higher-risk investments. At this point,
by definition, every short-term and long-term goal has already
been met. We've seen very few people reach this step of investing. Many who have don't like to speculate because they don't
want to risk the loss. They're more interested in preserving their
assets than accumulating more.

Let us repeat that advancing along this Investment Hierarchy is totally dependent upon your having a positive cash
flow margin. As you have surplus, the first priority use of that
cash is level 1, and so forth in sequence. You may even decide
to do your investing concurrently rather than sequentially. We
believe levels 1 and 2 must be met first, but then levels 3, 4,
and 5 could be met concurrently with your cash flow margin.
For example, you should try to take advantage of any employer

retirement plan that matches your contribution as soon as you can do so.

If you have an adequate emergency savings, you're better able to withstand the economic storms. The same is true if you have less debt, which we'll explore in the next chapter.

## CHAPTER 8

# I'M BEING EATEN BY THE BORROW CONSTRICTOR

## Step 5: Avoid Debt

If you owe money, be thankful you live in modern times rather than in ancient civilizations. In long-ago India and Nepal, creditors would "fast on" debtors, according to Dr. Charles Tabb, a University of Illinois law professor who specializes in bankruptcy. Creditors would go on a hunger strike on the debtor's doorway until the debt was paid. This was humiliating for the debtor's family and neighbors to see. If the creditor died while fasting, the rest of the community would take the debtor out and beat him to death.[21]

In ancient Greece, defaulting debtors would lose their citizenship. In many other cultures, those who couldn't repay debts were enslaved or sent to debtors' prison. Although current methods are not so extreme, being in debt does result in a type of bondage—at least, mental and emotional bondage, and maybe even staying in a job that feels like slavery.

Our society winks at debt today. It's so casual and easy to slip into—like well-worn slippers. Yet in financially fragile times, indebtedness can imperil our survival. Think about it. Could you continue to meet your financial obligations—car payments, credit card bills, installment loans, and the like—if you lost your job? What if an investment suddenly soured? What if you were offered a promising job opportunity—remember Denise and Mark? Would debt hold you back from taking it? Our economy may decline, but those who are out of debt are affected less.

In this chapter we will view debt through the window of economic uncertainty. We'll look for answers to questions such as: Is it ever okay to borrow money? How much debt can your financial structure support? These days, can anyone really afford a debt-free lifestyle? How do you get out of debt?

The answers will enable you to approach debt with a proper perspective. Debt doesn't have to threaten your economic comfort or survival. Debt may be a monster, but it's a beast you can tame.

## Don't End Up on a Debt-End Street

Today we tend to use terms such as *credit, borrow,* and *debt* almost interchangeably. There is, however, a difference between the three. You have credit when someone gives you the right to borrow money. When you exercise this right, you actually

---

**7 STEPS TO TAKE IF YOU'RE BEHIND ON YOUR HOUSE PAYMENTS**

1. Contact your lender immediately to work out a plan; don't wait several months to call.

2. See if you can change the terms to make payments more manageable.

3. Be alert to foreclosure rescue scams (see http://www.occ.treas.gov/ftp/advisory/2008-1.html for more information).

4. Contact a housing counseling service, which offers advice on foreclosures, defaults, and credit issues, for assistance (some are free). For a list of agencies approved by the U.S. Department of Housing and Urban Development, visit http://www.hud.gov/offices/hsg/sfh/hcc/hccprof14.cfm.

5. Cut back on all discretionary spending.

6. Take on extra jobs to increase income.

7. Treat your house payment as your most important bill.

borrow the money. And, until you are able to repay your obligations in full, you are in debt.

Being in debt doesn't seem to bother most consumers today. Chuck routinely borrows to buy vehicles costing nearly four to five times what his grandparents spent to build a new house in the 1950s. Maria charges a new designer outfit to reward herself for whittling her credit card balance down to $3,000. Total U.S. consumer debt, which includes credit card debt and non–credit card (but not mortgage) debt, reached $2.55 trillion at the end of 2007.[22] That's with a *"t"—trillion.* The solicitations continue: "Buy now and save! Make no payments until next March!"

We're not saying debt is wrong. Businesses often must borrow. Almost everyone must borrow to purchase their own house. Yet borrowing money has its price. That price is not just the interest rate. Anytime you use credit to borrow money, you precommit your future income. The effects of such obligations can range from simple inconvenience to financial devastation. Let's look at some of those consequences in more detail.

## "I Owe, I Owe, It's Off to Work I Go"

Money borrowed today must be repaid tomorrow. If you use credit to purchase an item now, counting on future income to make good on your promise to pay, you'll inevitably encounter one, if not both, of the following consequences:

1. You will have reduced freedom in the future. Mentally, emotionally, and financially, you will not experience the comfort level you could have known had you not precommitted your resources. Opportunity will knock, but you may not be free to answer the door.

2. You will face built-in constraints by financial decisions you make today. Every spending plan comes with ready-made restrictions based on individual spending and savings goals. Indebtedness only adds to the restrictions.

Like the proverbial monkey on your back, the money you owe will always be there to dictate your decisions and remind you of what you can and cannot do.

If you want to prepare yourself for an economically uncertain future, it stands to reason that you'll want to operate from a position of strength. Emotional and financial freedom from debt gives you strength. Opportunities may present themselves in prosperous times, yet they seem more available when times are tough and people panic. You'll want to take advantage of your options as you spot them.

Here are two desired outcomes to keep in mind as you work to strengthen your financial position:

- Maximize your flexibility.
- Minimize your constraints.

They are really two sides of the same coin. As you aim to follow these maxims, remember that an option that makes good sense from a strictly economic standpoint may not actually be a wise move. For example, one of my (Ron's) daughters and her husband lived in Nashville, Tennessee, when he was in graduate school. Just before the birth of their first child, they had an opportunity to purchase a condominium with monthly mortgage payments of $435—just $20 per month more than they were paying in rent on their one-bedroom apartment. They certainly needed the added space, and the property was selling below appraisal.

Economically, the purchase made sense. Yet as my daughter told me, they did not know how long they planned to stay in Nashville. Even though they could probably resell the condominium, they didn't want to obligate themselves in a way that might limit their future options.

## The Benefits of Debt-Free Living

If borrowing money limits financial flexibility, the absence of debt makes for a lifestyle of freedom and opportunity. With no, or even low, financial obligations, you will be at liberty to pursue your goals and desires.

I (Ron) once spoke with a man who had earned a hefty paycheck as a successful salesman. His desire, though, was to become involved in full-time Christian ministry. Having heard me speak on the benefits of debt-free living, he and his wife decided to pay off all their debts and start living within their income.

Soon the fellow realized his heart's desire when he accepted a position with Focus on the Family, which is where I met him. He told me that he and his wife now lived on a salary that was half of what he had made in sales. Yet thanks to their controlled spending and lack of debt, they actually had more money and greater financial freedom than ever before!

Freedom from the financial obligations of debt can mean the difference in how much can be given to charity. IRS statistics indicate that Americans pay nearly three times as much in mortgage interest as they give to charity.[23]

Getting rid of any debt—whether it's a large home mortgage or a relatively small credit card balance—is a guaranteed profitable investment. For example, if you use credit cards to borrow $2,000 to finance Christmas purchases, an annual vacation, or even just run-of-the-mill spending, you will incur an interest cost of around 18 percent. If you repay it by making only the seemingly easy minimum monthly payments, it will take you 32 years to do the job. You will ultimately spend $8,000 in interest, over and above the $2,000 principal!

If, on the other hand, you immediately repay the $2,000, you will, from an investment standpoint, actually save $8,000. You're even better off if you use your own cash to make the purchases in the first place. You won't need to worry about the possibility of paying interest that is four times greater than the actual amount borrowed.

## The Bullet-Point Version of a Debt Perspective

I (Ron) have provided free information about working out debt problems at the Web site www.masteryourmoney.com. There you can also read about other books dealing with debt and receive free answers to your common debt questions. This book is meant to be a quicker read, but many of the books and materials listed on the Web site contain debt worksheets and detailed information on managing and getting out of debt.

For now, we'd like to pass along our big-picture view of debt, which is based on a spiritual, as well as a financial, perspective.

Our key beliefs:

- Borrowing is not a sin.
- Borrowing may deny God an opportunity to work.
- Borrowing always presumes upon the future.
- Excessive borrowing may lead to financial bondage.
- Debt may be symptomatic of spiritual problems.
- Consumptive borrowing will sentence one to a reduced lifestyle in the future and will also limit financial flexibility and future financial independence.
- Husbands and wives should be in agreement when making debt decisions.
- Single individuals should check with a trusted friend or financial advisor about debt decisions.

When you're considering going into debt, ask yourself the following gut-check questions:

- Does assuming this debt make economic sense? In other words, will the economic return be greater than the economic cost?
- Do I have a guaranteed way to repay this debt?
- Do my spouse and I have unity in this decision?
- Do I have peace of mind when I consider making this borrowing decision?

- Do I have peace of mind when I pray through this borrowing decision?
- What personal goals and values am I meeting that can be met in no other way?
- What are my motives for assuming this debt?

We've both been in debt before but are out of debt now. We like being out much better than being in. You must handle debt with care. Going into debt is dangerous on several fronts:

- Financial:
  > Compounding works against you when you're in debt because you are charged interest, not only on the principal amount you borrowed, but also on the total amount (principal plus interest charges and other fees) you now owe.
  > If you're math minded, think of it this way. Simple interest is like addition: $2 + 2 + 2 + 2 + 2 = 10$. Compounded interest is like multiplication: $2 \times 2 \times 2 \times 2 \times 2 = 32$.
  > Getting in debt is easier than getting out. You pay back debt with after-tax dollars. So to repay a debt of $4,000, you have to earn $5,333 of income if you're in the 25 percent income tax bracket.
  > Debt limits the future.

- Spiritual:
  > Debt presumes upon the future. Specifically, when going into debt, you may assume that because you earn a good income or your house should go up in value, borrowing does not carry any risk for you. However, if your presumptions don't work out— you're laid off or your house declines in value—you may find yourself in financial bondage.
  > It may deny God an opportunity to provide. God wants to increase our faith; He has also promised

to meet all our needs. In many cases, however, borrowing money prevents God from either meeting our needs or showing Himself faithful, which in turn prevents our faith from increasing.

> Debt may limit opportunities to serve God. Income that must go to repay debts cannot be channeled to giving or service and educational opportunities.

- Psychological:
  > A family's stress level, particularly the wife's, increases with debt. Even if you have a plan to get out of debt, something in the back of your mind always wonders, *How will I repay?*

- Reputation:
  > Your reputation and testimony suffer if you are unable to repay or are forced into bankruptcy.

## Living Together in Unity

For married couples, many debt temptations may be avoided by adhering to one of marriage's built-in safeguards; that is, the differing perspectives that husbands and wives have on financial matters.

We believe God puts men and women together to complement and complete one another. Psalm 133:1 (NKJV) says, "How good and how pleasant it is for brethren to dwell together in unity!" Applying this principle to marriage and money, we submit that borrowing decisions should never be made without the full consent of both spouses.

Every year couples seeking advice on a potential investment tell us about hundreds of "great deals." In almost every case, the deal promoter is the husband. The wife is typically more reserved; she is far less willing to risk losing their capital than her scheme-happy or entrepreneurial husband. (Exceptions exist, of course, but these are my general observations.)

**THE 6 MOST IMPORTANT STEPS TO BEGIN
DIGGING YOURSELF OUT OF DEBT**

1. Admit that changes need to be made.

2. Determine the real reason the debt occurred.

3. Determine where you currently are financially.

4. Consider what steps you can take or have taken to keep from going into debt again.

5. Develop a repayment plan.

6. Reduce your living expenses to halt the accumulation of debt and free up money for debt repayment.

When we speak to men on this subject, we urge them to follow two rules:

1. If you cannot explain an investment or a need for debt to your wife so she can understand it, you do not understand the situation well enough to make the investment or incur the debt.

2. If you can and do explain a potential financial move to your wife and she does not feel good about it, do not pursue it.

I (Ron) spent years failing to apply these two rules in my communication with my wife, Judy. As a result, I missed the counsel of a very wise person. Like many men, I assumed that because my wife was not a CPA and had no formal training in finance or economics, she could not understand all of our financial circumstances. The truth is, women often have an intuitive sense that men lack—especially concerning money matters and debt. Wisdom does not always require intellectual understanding. Consider the example of Abigail, whose story is told in 1 Samuel 25.

Abigail and her husband, Nabal, made an interesting pair. She was beautiful and intelligent; he was surly, wicked, and foolish. Nabal was also very wealthy, owning a large number of sheep and goats.

The soon-to-be-king David and his men had protected Nabal's shepherds as they went about their work. At sheep-shearing time, David sent messengers to ask Nabal for some sort of hospitality in return. Scoffing at the request, Nabal refused. When David heard Nabal's response, he mounted an attack, intending to kill Nabal and all of his men.

When Abigail learned what had happened, she immediately set about straightening things out. Packing a feast for six hundred men, she rode out to meet David's war party. She humbly begged David's pardon and advised him to avoid vindication, which could weaken his future standing as king. Impressed by her good judgment, David called off the attack.

Abigail probably knew little about Nabal's business dealings, and she certainly did not share David's experience as a warrior. Yet thanks to her sensible actions and wise words, she protected both men.

Like many women, Abigail did not need intellectual understanding or personal experience to make a smart move. She intuitively knew what to say and do. David recognized this and benefited greatly from her advice. Nabal, on the other hand, did not even consider discussing the matter with his wife. And when he finally did grasp the significance of what had happened, he had some sort of heart attack and died.

We want to challenge men to be like David instead of Nabal and listen to their wives. Although we're both accountants and financial advisors, we seek our wives' advice. As a result, we're confident that we're making better decisions.

The need for spousal unity is just one of the principles God offers to enable us to use credit wisely. Other safeguards are all around us, from biblical references on borrowing to the other books written on the subject. Learning to follow the principles in this chapter will probably mean you can't have everything you want whenever you want it. What you will

have, though, is a better treasure by far—the peace of mind
that comes from knowing you are on the right path no matter
what the future brings.

If you are saddled with debt, your financial situation will
control you. On the other hand, if you practice wise stewardship
and remain unhindered by debt's bondage, you will be in better
control. You will be free to look to the Lord to supply guidance,
direction, and peace, regardless of the uncontrolled and uncon-
trollable economic future of our nation and world.

## CHAPTER 9

# HONEY, I'VE SHRUNK OUR PORTFOLIO!

## Step 6: Think Long Term with Investing

During the tumultuous month of September 2008, well-respected names in the financial community teetered. Some fell; some were rescued by government assistance, including a $700 billion bailout package. The world stock markets dropped. Ratings for the cable business news channels soared. The financial experts trotted over to Washington to testify in hearings.

The well-respected *Wall Street Journal* is not prone to sensationalism or tabloid-type reporting. Yet during the week of September 15, it printed some troubling headlines—in a font much larger and much bolder than its typical headlines.

**Shock Hits World Markets[24]**

**US Plans Rescue of AIG to Halt Crisis; Central Banks Inject Cash as Credit Dries Up[25]**

**Mounting Fears Shake World Markets as Banking Giants Rush to Find Buyers[26]**

**Worst Crisis Since 30's, with No End in Sight[27]**

**In Turmoil, Capitalism in U.S. Sets New Course[28]**

Just look at the frightening words in large font: *shock, crisis, fears, turmoil.* Indeed, it was—and continues to be—a challenging time. You would think from these headlines that the stock market tanked and chalked up its worst week ever. On Friday's close, however, the Dow Jones Industrial Average had ended the week nearly unchanged, just 33.55 points lower than when the "crisis" started![29]

If you were on vacation in a remote place during that week without the 24-7 news coverage of the "crisis," your investment portfolio wouldn't have been much lower when you returned. But if you stayed home and tracked the market on the Internet or on cable news channels, you likely developed an ulcer. This proves the old saying, "The stock market can be like a roller coaster. You end up where you started, but feel worse from it."

Because investing causes more fear than most other aspects of personal finance, we're focusing this chapter on developing a practical and personal investment strategy.

## The No-Brainer Investment

When people ask our advice on personal investments, we automatically ask them if their employers offer a pension, profit-sharing plan, 401(k), or 403(b) plan into which they can make voluntary contributions.

Most people's first long-term investments come in the form of company-sponsored retirement plans. They may be called a thrift plan, profit-sharing plan, defined contribution plan, 401(k) plan, money purchase plan, or a SIMPLE IRA plan. A common characteristic is that they allow an employee to contribute pretax dollars (dollars that are deducted from an individual's paycheck before taxes are calculated) that will grow tax deferred until retirement.

Remember our explanation of why compounding hurts you when you've borrowed money? (If not, see page 81.) Investments, including retirement plans, use compounding to your

**7 THINGS *NOT* TO DO WHEN THE STOCK MARKET HAS CUT YOUR RETIREMENT FUND IN HALF**

1. Move everything to cash if you have a long time horizon—this merely locks in the on-paper losses.

2. Cash in the account if you're under 59½, since you'll have to pay a 10 percent penalty plus taxes.

3. Stop adding to your accounts regularly.

4. Listen to neighbors and friends instead of your financial advisor.

5. Listen to rumors that cause panic.

6. Lose patience.

7. Avoid your financial advisor.

advantage since you earn a return both on the contributions to the plan, as well as the return they've already earned. Furthermore, many employers also contribute and/or match funds to their employees' retirement plans.

Contributing to a 401(k) or IRA, therefore, is almost always a good strategy. However, before making other long-term investments, you should be sure you've (1) eliminated all credit card and consumer debt and (2) established your emergency fund. Whether your investments currently are limited to funds in an employer-sponsored retirement plan or your investments go beyond that, you need to have the right approach to investing.

## Developing Your Own "Fiscalosophy"

When consulting with clients about their investments, we often find that they have never created a personal philosophy of investing. We're not suggesting that every philosophy of investing should be the same. However, we've tried to base our philosophy of investing on biblical principles. As shown in the following chart, the biblical perspective is much different than the worldly perspective.

## Biblical versus Worldly Perspective

| Biblical Perspective | Worldly Perspective |
|---|---|
| Preservation and steady growth of capital (Proverbs 28:20) | Get rich quick |
| Long-time horizon (Luke 14:28) | Short-time horizon |
| Save/invest first (Proverbs 24:27; Ecclesiastes 5:13-14) | Spend/consume quickly |
| Time is a tool (Proverbs 6:6; 28:22) | Time is an enemy |
| Cycles are inevitable (2 Peter 3:4) | Upward trend hopeful |
| Diversification strategy (Ecclesiastes 11:2) | Timing strategy |

The primary source of wealth or capital for most people comes from accumulation and multiplication of one's surplus. Remember that this surplus (or cash flow margin) is simply the difference between one's income and expenses. (Although a few people may receive an inheritance, life insurance proceeds, or a settlement, most individuals must pull dollars for investing from their annual cash flow margin.) The surplus must be consistently positive in order to accomplish one's long-term objectives.

We've observed that it's harder to keep wealth than it is to earn it. Many of our clients earned their income through sophisticated technical and vocational skills. However, very few of them had the professional expertise in investments to know how to build that wealth and make it grow over a period of time. Therefore, we tend to view capital preservation (not losing the accumulated investments) as a much higher priority than earning the highest yield or greatest growth of capital.

Because a person's resources are always limited, certain things must be traded off. The classical trade-off is between risk and reward. It is impossible to consistently buy high-quality investments at low prices. Therefore, you can't expect that the yield on high-quality investments will be equal to the yield on high-risk, low-quality investments. You have safety in exchange for reduction in yield. Or to receive a potentially high rate of return, you must put up with market fluctuations.

If you keep a long-term perspective, you have time to compound modest yields. You no longer have to try to predict the future regarding the tops and bottoms of market and economic cycles. Fear-based decisions, especially in the short term, lead to poor, irrational decisions.

The short version of our fiscalosophy:[30] Develop a positive cash flow margin. Invest for the long term through a diversified portfolio. Keep a long-term, sustainable stewardship mind-set. God cares where and how you invest His resources. We'd like for you to develop your own fiscalosophy. Let us help you begin that process by focusing on your tendencies.

## Pinpointing Your Personal Paradigm

A paradigm sounds like a fifty-cent consultant-type word. We suppose it is. But a paradigm reflects your assumptions and biases in how you will interpret any given experience. Your paradigm influences your perspective. From a financial standpoint, two common paradigms drive most investment decisions of the two different types of investors: fear-based investors and effective investors.

Which one are you? One way to accurately assess your personal paradigm is to measure how it affects your decision-making process. Fear-based and effective investors are marked by two very different mind-sets:

### Two Types of Investors

| Fear-Based Investor | Effective Investor |
| --- | --- |
| Reactive | Proactive |
| Blind | Visionary |
| Hoarder | Generous |

## Are You Reactive or Proactive?

Let's say that Jay invested in a start-up company that became successful initially. Within months, Jay saw his initial investment jump 10 times in value. He was ecstatic! Shortly thereafter, though, the stock price dropped to where Jay's investment was worth only 20 percent more than its original value. Most investors would be pleased with this net gain in a relatively short time. Yet all Jay could see was the loss. Gripped by fear, Jay began hoarding his wealth. His entire mood depended upon an upturn in the price of his stock, which he monitored almost constantly.

Jay is reactive. His emotions and investment decisions are driven by market fluctuations. In other words, he's a thermometer (see page 18).

If you're proactive, on the other hand, you expect market highs and lows. You're content to monitor your investments monthly or even quarterly. With an effective investment strategy in place, you take responsibility for your decisions. You don't fall victim to fear or the temptation to blame others for your losses.

Are you like Jay? Take the following quiz to measure your reactive or proactive position. Be honest with yourself and circle the number, 1 to 5, that best reflects how much you disagree (1) or agree (5) with each statement. (Note: This test and others in this chapter are not meant to peg you with a "right" or "wrong" label. Rather, you can use your scores as simple indicators of where your paradigm lies and then consider whether you need to make a paradigm shift.)

### Reactive versus Proactive Investors

If an investment drops in value, I have a hard time giving or spending any money; instead, I want to hang on to what I have left.

1     2     3     4     5

I check my investment positions weekly, if not daily, so I will know when to make a move.

1     2     3     4     5

I tend to blame others—my broker, my spouse, other investors—for my market losses.

1    2    3    4    5

I get nervous "riding" the market; when stock prices start to dip I want to jump ship.

1    2    3    4    5

I cannot predict the future, so I watch the market fluctuations for investment clues and make my decisions accordingly.

1    2    3    4    5

Total your score: _____

5–11: Your proactive approach will go far toward making you an effective investor.
12–17: You are in the neutral zone. Watch for more clues to determine your personal paradigm.
18–25: Your reactive tendencies may make you lean toward the fear-based mentality.

## Are You Blind or Visionary?

Once there was a man who, before embarking on a long journey, called together his servants. In this servant meeting, he entrusted his assets to them. One servant received the equivalent of about five thousand dollars. Another servant received two thousand; the third was given one thousand.

While their master was gone, the first two servants invested the master's money. They each doubled their portions. The third fellow, however, was afraid to take any chances. Digging a hole, he hid his one thousand dollars safely in the ground.

When the master returned and discovered what had happened, he praised and promoted the two moneymaking men. The third servant, though, found himself stripped of his resources and his responsibilities. In his master's eyes he was wicked, lazy, and just plain stupid.

This story, told by Jesus and recorded in Matthew 25:14-30, illustrates two investment outlooks. The visionary investor deftly balances risks and rewards to identify worthy investment opportunities. The blind investor is crippled by the fear of accepting even a small degree of risk. He chooses to hoard his limited assets where he thinks they will be safe.

Blindness can also strike in the opposite form—an inability to see any risk. Throwing caution to the wind, the blind investor may plunge headlong into any investment that promises a payoff—from shrimp futures to Brazilian opal mines.

Are you blind or visionary? Consider this test a financial eye examination. Circle the number, 1 to 5, that reflects how much you disagree (1) or agree (5) with each statement.

**Blind versus Visionary Investors**
I am only interested in "guaranteed" investment deals.

1     2     3     4     5

I am apt to follow a "hot tip" if it sounds like a big moneymaker.

1     2     3     4     5

I like to keep my money in the bank or in relatively secure money market funds.

1     2     3     4     5

Brazilian opal mines sound good to me; after all, long odds offer the biggest payoff.

1     2     3     4     5

I tend to view an investment as either risky or rewarding, but not both.

1     2     3     4     5

Total your score: _____

5–11: You probably have the vision necessary for effective investing.

12–17: Invest with caution, taking care to weigh all risks and rewards.
18–25: Stay away from the market—at least until you get a good pair of eyeglasses!

All investors are either accumulating wealth or working to preserve it. Neither phase benefits from a hoarding or reckless paradigm. The best investors use their proactive and visionary abilities to plot and follow a strategic course to financial success.

## Three Key Factors for Preserving Investments

Just as the sages of real estate investing emphasize location, location, location, preserving your investments depends on three factors: diversification, diversification, diversification. When the roller coaster of the economy zooms on the big hills, diversification is the way you hang on. It's your seat belt and safety bar. Solomon, in his wisdom, offers an excellent investment strategy in Ecclesiastes 11:2: "Divide your portion to seven, or even to eight, for you do not know what misfortune may occur on the earth" (NASB).

Diversification is spreading your money among different types of investments. By doing so, you diminish your overall risk.

A retired couple wanted to start a small business in the mountains of North Carolina. They were leaning toward opening a cozy gourmet coffee shop. Then a friend pointed out that the coffee shop would be a welcome retreat from the brisk autumn breezes and winter snows, but sales were apt to be sluggish during the hot summer months. (This was before Starbucks made iced lattes and Frappuccinos a staple of such businesses.)

Rethinking their plan, the couple decided to open a coffee and ice cream shop. When coffee sales lagged in the heat, ice cream would lure the summertime crowds. Similarly a hot cup of coffee would keep the winter customers coming even if ice cream sales melted. By diversifying their offerings, the couple had hit

95

## 10 MOST COMMON INVESTMENT MISTAKES

1. Having no goals

2. Ignoring counsel of spouse

3. Listening to friends and family on what stocks to buy

4. Trying to get rich quick

5. Ignoring the risk/reward relationship (see page 90)

6. Borrowing for an investment

7. Failing to diversify

8. Failing to use a competent, trusted financial advisor

9. Investing before paying off credit card and consumer debt

10. Failing to understand investments before making them

upon a plan that would reduce their overall risk while enhancing their total return.

The most important strategy affecting the preservation of capital is a diversified portfolio. In other words, people must spread their investments among several alternatives so that if any of them suffers, the entire investment portfolio does not shrink. Obviously the trade-off is to give up the potential for hitting it big in a single investment for a modest return on the entire investment portfolio.

## Diversification Process

Most stocks and bonds took a hit in the 2008 economic downturn. A common question became "Why diversify if international stocks, U.S. stocks, and bonds all went down?" Diversification doesn't guarantee a better return, but it reduces risk.

What is the best way to spread out or diversify investments? A study by Citigroup found that to minimize stock-specific risks, a portfolio would need a minimum of 25 to 30 stocks.[31] This is not practical for most people to do on their own.

Each transaction has a cost, and the amount of money needed would be too high. Besides, which 30 stocks would you pick? A better way to diversify is to invest in mutual funds. Mutual funds are professionally managed and hold hundreds of stocks.

Investing in just one mutual fund—rather than buying a single stock—will diversify your portfolio. Just ask the people who invested only in the stock of AIG, Lehman Brothers, Enron, MCI WorldCom, or many other failed companies (often these investors were also company employees). If their money had been in a mutual fund rather than in a single company's stock, their losses would have been much less.

Although a mutual fund is certainly more diversified than a few stocks, you can diversify even further. We suggest diversifying on multiple levels as shown below. By moving from one category to the next, investors have the ability to diversify within diversification, thereby strengthening the total portfolio.

## DIVERSIFICATION HIERARCHY

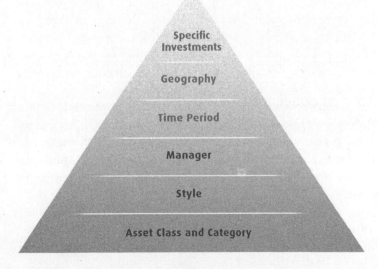

Specific Investments

Geography

Time Period

Manager

Style

Asset Class and Category

## The Diversification Hierarchy

Let's go a bit deeper in explaining each of the steps of this diversification hierarchy.

**Diversification by asset class and category.** This is the most widely practiced form of diversification. Think of it as combining different assets—such as stocks, bonds, international investments, and real estate—into a single portfolio. These various assets have different risk and return potential. So they rise and fall in value at different rates from one another. By combining two or more asset classes, you can reduce the volatility, or risk, in the portfolio.

Asset categories are a subgroup of asset classes. A smart diversification strategy includes investments in different categories within each asset class. The chart on page 99 highlights asset classes and categories, and offers some common examples in each category.

**Diversification by investment style.** An investment style is the strategy used for buying and selling investments. Different investment styles, including value style, growth style, quantitative analysis, and index funds, become popular at different times, just as different fashions come in vogue from time to time. During the bull market of the late 1990s, the growth style was very popular as growth stocks led the market for several years. Growth style is selecting companies whose earnings are likely to grow quickly, such as Amazon.com or Google.

Then, when the market endured losses in the early 2000s, the value style performed much better than growth. A value style looks for companies whose stock is trading below the value of their assets or business. A value-style manager looks for bargains or turnaround opportunities. Examples may include a utility or a bank.

The best-diversified portfolios incorporate a combination of two or more investment styles at all times. Try to avoid chasing the most recent popular style. Doing what the crowd does

## Examples of Asset Classes and Categories

| Asset Class | Category | Example |
|---|---|---|
| Stocks | Large company | Dow Jones industrials, blue chips |
| | Small company | NASDAQ, speculative |
| International | Developed markets | Germany, Great Britain, Japan |
| | Emerging/ developing markets | Mexico, Chile, Singapore, Thailand |
| Bonds | Government | Treasury notes/bills, Series EE |
| | Corporate | Bonds, debentures |
| | Municipal | Airport authority, county revenue, and sales tax |
| | Speculative | Junk, international, mortgage |
| | Mortgage pools | GNMA, FNMA |
| Real estate | Income-producing | Apartment complex, building space |
| | Non-income-producing | Raw land |
| | Stocks | REITs |
| Precious metals | Gold and silver | Krugerrands, coins, bars |

may work well in picking a good restaurant, but not in picking good investments. Different styles perform differently in various scenarios. Investing purely in one style, even if other diversification methods are used, will still expose you to unnecessary risks.

**Diversification by manager.** Within each asset class and investment style an investor can diversify by relying on several different managers (or funds with different managers). Each manager has his or her own biases and blind spots. Using several managers (or funds) reduces the risk of a portfolio's being severely damaged by the poor performance of any one individual.

**Diversification over time.** This diversification approach has two strategies: one used for fixed-income investments and one that works with growth-oriented investments.

Fixed-income investments, such as bonds or CDs, benefit from staggered maturity dates, which reduce the interest rate risk. You'd hate to be locked into one five-year bond or CD and then watch interest rates rise significantly in year two. So buy several bonds or CDs lasting different periods. In a retirement plan, you may have mutual funds investing in bonds. Spread your investments among short-term, intermediate-term, and long-term bond funds.

Dollar cost averaging is the second time-diversification strategy. The idea behind dollar cost averaging is that when you invest a regular amount of money in a particular stock or mutual fund on a regular basis, your potential for receiving a gain when you sell improves. More on this later in the chapter.

**Diversification by geography.** International investments offer geographic diversification. Emerging markets in lesser developed countries may offer excellent growth potential. Developed countries may offer additional opportunities separate from the U.S. markets.

## The Diversification Disclaimer

Remember, diversification reduces risk. It doesn't offer the greatest potential return or offer a guaranteed return. Here's the oft-repeated observation in wealth management circles: "To build wealth, concentrate; to preserve wealth, diversify."

To achieve the greatest amount of wealth (and take more

risk), investors concentrate their investment holdings. Bill Gates built his wealth by concentrating his portfolio on Microsoft; Sam Walton, on Wal-Mart. To keep their billions, these men had regular programs to sell company stock and then diversified to preserve their wealth. We've offered a big-picture view with lots of technical information. It's hard to achieve the diversification hierarchy by yourself. We recommend that you use the services of a qualified financial advisor you can trust. I (Ron) work with many outstanding advisors through Kingdom Advisors. You can find a Kingdom Advisor in your area by going to www.kingdomadvisors.org.

Although it's implied, we didn't include in the Diversification Hierarchy another area to diversify: "away from employer." This means to invest your 401(k) or stock portfolio in other companies besides your employer. In the late 1990s and early 2000s, my (Ron's) firm consulted with Enron executives and suggested they reduce their company stock holdings. Many had 100 percent Enron stock in their portfolios. They initially thought my recommendation was wrong because Enron was such a well-regarded, high-flying stock. After Enron filed bankruptcy and the stock was worthless, the principle of diversification looked attractive to those who had lost most of their savings.

When we suggest, "Don't hold company stock in your 401(k)," our aim is to reduce your risk. You're already dependent upon your employer for your current earnings, health insurance, and pension. Why tie up more of your wealth by investing in company stock?

## How Much Courage Do You Have? Buy When Low

Do you want to know a secret? Successful investors buy low and sell high. Duh, no surprise there. The secret is how to implement that buy-low and sell-high method consistently over time. Academic studies have found that no one can time the market accurately over long periods of time. Anyone can get lucky on occasion.

Investors in the stock market or mutual funds have learned that the market can go in one of three directions: up, down, or sideways. But not even the experts can consistently choose the correct direction.

The future of the market is an unknown. It always has been and always will be. With that in mind, is there a method of investing that reduces risk for the individual amateur investor while producing consistent results? Good news: there is! The method is called dollar cost averaging. That's the secret.

Dollar cost averaging is simply investing the same amount of money in a mutual fund or stock at regular intervals over a long period of time. Let's look at three simple illustrations. Suppose you have $1,500 to invest. You can choose either to put all of it in an investment at once or make five equal installments.

### Declining Market

| Regular Investment | Share Price | Shares Acquired |
|---|---|---|
| $300 | 25 | 12 |
| $300 | 15 | 20 |
| $300 | 20 | 15 |
| $300 | 10 | 30 |
| $300 | 5 | 60 |
| Total: $1,500 | 75 | 137 |

Average price paid per share ($75 ÷ 5) = $15.00
Dollar cost averaging price per share ($1,500 ÷ 137) = $10.95

As you can see, the discipline of dollar cost averaging forces you to buy more shares when they are the cheapest. Any recovery above the dollar cost average price of $10.95 produces a profit. You are in an excellent position for a market recovery. If you had invested the entire $1,500 at $25/share, the market would have had to go above $25/share before you realized a profit. You could have had a long wait!

## Steady Market

| Regular Investment | Share Price | Shares Acquired |
|---|---|---|
| $300 | 12 | 25 |
| $300 | 15 | 20 |
| $300 | 12 | 25 |
| $300 | 15 | 20 |
| $300 | 12 | 25 |
| Total:    $1,500 | 66 | 115 |

Average price paid per share ($66 ÷ 5) = $13.20
Dollar cost averaging price per share ($1,500 ÷ 115) = $13.04

Not much difference exists here, but remember you have achieved slightly better results by spreading out your investments, thereby taking less risk.

## Rising Market

| Regular Investment | Share Price | Shares Acquired |
|---|---|---|
| $300 | 5 | 60 |
| $300 | 15 | 20 |
| $300 | 10 | 30 |
| $300 | 15 | 20 |
| $300 | 25 | 12 |
| Total:    $1,500 | 70 | 142 |

Average price paid per share ($70 ÷ 5) = $14.00
Dollar cost averaging price per share ($1,500 ÷ 142) = $10.56

In a rising market, dollar cost averaging provides a limit to market exposure. You buy fewer shares when they are expensive or overvalued.

Three conditions help dollar cost averaging to work:

1. The stock market fluctuates.
2. Over a long period of time, the stock market will generally trend upward.
3. You are taking a disciplined approach and can resist the temptation to take short-term gains or succumb to panic selling in declining markets.

After a declining market, dollar cost averaging can position you for handsome gains because you own more shares at the lowest average cost. In a rising market, dollar cost averaging provides positive returns. In all three types of market, you have not exposed 100 percent of your principal to the market, but rather have been earning interest in money market funds on the uninvested balance.

The drawback to dollar cost averaging? It's so simple and structured that you can't brag to your friends about how shrewd you are! Dollar cost averaging doesn't tell you when to sell, but it provides a systematic buying process.

## Is All That Glitters Gold?

In times of economic uncertainty, people begin considering gold investments. When times are good, gloom-and-doom naysayers say to buy gold because uncertain times are coming. We recommend a balanced approach between the "gold bugs" who think that gold is the only investment a person should pursue and those who don't like gold and silver because of their unexciting nature and the discipline it takes to buy and hold them. With any investment, a balanced approach is best.

As part of a diversified portfolio, we think gold has a place. A small place. We don't think that gold and silver should comprise more than 5 percent of your total portfolio. Don't add it to your portfolio until you've taken care of the other steps in this book. In other words, it's one of the last, refining steps to polish off your portfolio.

Two strategies come to mind when purchasing gold and silver. The first strategy is buying and trading it for investment purposes. Our advice is to avoid this. I (Ron) have several friends who lost money during the silver run-up of the late 1970s. With a tenfold increase, people became crazed with the excitement of potential profits.

For the vast majority of readers, however, trading in gold and silver does not make sense. Novices are no match against professionals who control this volatile and active market.

The second strategy is to buy gold as a "wealth preserver." This is a valid approach. Gold will protect your purchasing power in times of higher inflation. In the early 1900s you could have bought a man's dress suit for either a $20 gold coin or a $20 bill. Let's suppose you had that same $20 gold coin today and a $20 bill. The $20 gold coin would still allow you to buy the suit—probably the best one available—while the $20 bill probably would not even pay for a shirt. Gold has indeed preserved purchasing power through the years.

People can't counterfeit gold. Governments can't print more of it and devalue it. While the long-lasting purchasing power of gold is exciting, there's also a very unexciting side to gold and silver as an investment. It just sits there; it doesn't earn you any interest; you don't show it to your friends. You just hide it.

Years ago I (Ron) placed some of my hard-earned money in gold and silver. I then proceeded to watch the real estate market take off with inflation. After the real estate market cooled down, the stock market began its great bull surge in the early 1980s. Even the interest on my money market funds in many years outperformed gold and silver. More than once, I was tempted to switch into something that could earn more money. I had to remind myself constantly that I originally purchased it as a long-term investment and an inflation protector. In the last few years, my patience was rewarded.

## 10 Principles of Successful Investing

No matter who you are, you will make investment mistakes. I've made them too. If you have experienced market losses, then learn from them, move on, and forget them. Too often we beat ourselves up over bad decisions. Perhaps our spouses won't forget, or won't let us forget, our mistakes. Just as God forgives us for our sins—including poor stewardship—we should forgive ourselves (and maybe a spouse) as well.

To close this chapter on investing, we'd like to boil down investing wisdom into one chart. These principles work. We've seen them work to the advantage of many people in our careers. We've also seen how people have suffered when they've not followed these principles. These principles are technically sound, but more importantly they are based on principles in the Bible.

### 10 Biblical Principles of Successful Investing

| | |
|---|---|
| 1. Establish written financial goals | Proverbs 20:5; 21:5 |
| 2. Seek wise counsel | Proverbs 19:20 |
| 3. Cultivate a long-term perspective | Luke 14:28 |
| 4. Diversify your portfolio | Ecclesiastes 11:2 |
| 5. Strive for consistency; don't make haste to get rich quick | Proverbs 28:20, 22 |
| 6. Avoid risky investments if you can't afford the loss | Ecclesiastes 5:13-15 |
| 7. Avoid high leverage | Proverbs 22:7 |
| 8. Monitor your anxiety | Psalm 131:1 |
| 9. Establish limits on the amount you invest | Proverbs 15:16; 30:8 |
| 10. Share and discuss your decisions with your spouse | Genesis 2:24 |

# A FINAL WORD FROM THE AUTHORS

We've completed many radio interviews recently regarding the economic uncertainty facing our country. During these programs, we've fielded many calls from consumers worried about losing their homes or their jobs or who feel overwhelmed by their consumer debt. While your family's financial situation is different from every other's, everyone can apply the same basic principles to their situations and begin to take steps in the right direction.

Likewise, while the factors surrounding the latest round of economic turbulence are different from the ones before it, economic upheaval is not new. Throughout our careers, we have experienced many periods of economic uncertainty: wars and rumors of wars, the dot-com bust, recessionary times, the savings and loan crisis, the subprime mortgage and banking crisis, and more.

Whether in economically prosperous or difficult times, the principles presented in this book will work. They seem simple. Well, they are simple in the sense that they're straightforward. The answers to your challenges are not found only on Wall Street through a financially complex investment product. They're based on God's truth. That truth as revealed in the Bible is always relevant, always right, and will never change.

*For answers to more of your questions on spending plans, debt reduction, and more, visit www.masteryourmoney.com.*

*To learn more about Kingdom Advisors or find a financial advisor in your area, see www.kingdomadvisors.org.*

# 40 MONEY-SAVING TIPS

As we mentioned in chapter 6, you must spend less than you earn to meet your short- and long-term financial goals. To do that, you can either increase your earnings or reduce your expenses. Reducing expenses provides a dollar-for-dollar impact. Increasing your income does not. If you earn $150 more, then you have to pay $20 to $50 in taxes. Look first to reducing expenses before working longer and harder to pay the tax burden.

The following list is not meant to be exhaustive, but it does represent ideas our families have used or we've seen others follow to spend wisely and accomplish financial goals.

Many people are considered "cheap" if they are known to pursue bargains or seek out the most economical sources for products or services. In fact, often people who go to extreme lengths to save money on everything they buy are ridiculed by others who—when they need advice on where to shop to save money—ask the "cheapskates"! Why? Because deep down, even spendthrifts see the wisdom of saving every possible dollar in order to use it more productively.

1. **Buy used.** This is an especially good idea for major purchases. Contrary to popular belief, buying used is not risky and doesn't take a lot of expertise. It does take planning and a little bit of elbow grease.

   For example, a coworker of mine (Ron's) who relocated

to Atlanta needed to buy a refrigerator for his house. New refrigerators at that time cost about $750—way more than he had in cash after purchasing his first home. He decided that buying used was the best option. First, he studied refrigerators in *Consumer Reports* magazine. Second, he began scanning the classified ads and made a lot of telephone calls. After becoming more experienced at classified shopping, he learned how to screen people and determine who was overselling or hyping their merchandise and who had genuine reasons for wanting to sell what they owned.

Third, he limited his search to certain geographic and income areas of the city. He couldn't afford to drive all over a large metropolitan area in order to find that treasured refrigerator. He focused on nearby suburban areas. The result: he bought an almost new refrigerator for $250. Last check, it was still going strong nine years later. There was nothing wrong with the refrigerator except that it was the wrong color for the seller's new home!

One of the main points in buying used is that, if at all possible, you should anticipate your need. If you know you are going to need a new appliance or a car, begin shopping three or four months before replacement becomes necessary. Through the years we have bought many used items for our families: automobiles, ski equipment, televisions, furniture, children's clothing, and tools.

One of the most obvious items to buy used is an automobile. Studies indicate that new cars depreciate 20 to 40 percent in the first year of ownership. Let someone else pay for that depreciation! Used cars are more reliable today, and extended warranties are available, so the used car buyer runs much less risk than he or she did a few years ago.

Two quick tips for buying a used car: First, check out the car. There are services available through the Internet to trace the history of the car for recalls, if it's been involved in a wreck, etc. Consider having a mechanic check out any car you are serious about purchasing. The charge for this, perhaps $100 to $200, is well spent to avoid buying someone else's lemon. Second, try to buy from someone who can produce service records and who you feel has taken good care of his or her car. If you buy from a used car lot or dealer, ask if you can talk to the previous owner.

2. **Rent.** Some things you just don't need to own: vacation cottages, boats, major tools, recreational vehicles, and the list goes on. It's amazing how easy and cheap it is to rent something that is state of the art, return it when you want to, and not have to worry about maintenance, depreciation, storage, obsolescence, or property taxes.

For most people, the ownership of time-sharing or resort properties is a bad idea. Renting a vacation property that someone else owns is generally a better deal. A friend explained how each summer his family and other relatives rent a gorgeous $500,000 beach house for $850 per week. Each day as he lies on the deck taking in the sun, he says to himself, *This is great! I don't have to worry about painting or fixing it up during my stay here, and there's no depreciation, no property taxes, no worry about vandalism.* The owner has the worries, and this friend has the fun. He's controlling a $500,000 asset for $850 a week. Now that's leverage.

3. **Shop garage sales and children's clothing sales.** Garage sales are an excellent source for children's clothing. Shop in better neighborhoods and you can often (for a fraction of the original price) get brand-name clothing that has simply been outgrown. Many churches or entrepreneurial mothers have coordinated clothing sales; get on their mailing lists so you can attend those events. Why pay $35 in a store for a blue blazer that Johnny will outgrow in six months when you can buy it at a used clothing sale for $5?

4. **Membership warehouses.** In major metropolitan areas membership warehouses are popular. Offering no-frills

shopping and limited selection, prices are often only 5 percent above wholesale. If you know what you want and you can purchase in quantity, these offer an excellent value. By shopping in bulk, you can save on time and gas as you cut down on trips to stores. (Just be sure you're buying what you need—just because you *can* buy a 50-pack box of a snack item doesn't mean you *should* buy it. Also, some warehouse clubs offer brand names that may be higher priced—even when purchased in larger quantities—than generic or private label brands.)

5. **Comparison shop.** If you need to make a major purchase or have major repairs done on your car, get more than one estimate. The prices may vary by several hundred dollars. The same holds true for your annual auto insurance, phone service provider, and homeowner's insurance. Shop around. Your present company may be charging you higher rates than the competition without just reason. Keep them honest and compare costs every few years.

Nowadays, of course, the Internet has many comparison buying sites to help you compare the prices of anything from digital cameras to appliances to computers. A few popular sites are www.mysimon.com, www.shopping.yahoo.com, and shopping.com; eBay is a great resource to find out what items have recently sold for.

6. **Pay cash.** Paying cash offers two advantages. First, you can sometimes buy an item for less by offering cash instead of charging. Second, it is a lot harder to plunk down greenbacks than it is to use plastic; therefore, you more carefully "count the cost" of each purchase. (In fact, many studies confirm that those who pay with cash rather than a credit card spend less.)

7. **Generic brands.** Major grocery stores often offer generic or house brands. Don't be afraid of them! Many manufactur-

ers make both the brand-name and generic items. Often the ingredients are exactly the same; only the label is different. Juice is juice, salt is salt, bleach is bleach. It doesn't hurt to try a product once; then if you don't like it, you can go back to the brand name. But if you like it, you will save money, and that savings multiplied by a number of years and compounded can add up to significant future dollars.

8. **Wait on impulse or major purchases.** If you are in a store and that new flat-screen TV really looks appealing, the "justification juices" can start coursing through your veins. One good piece of advice is to wait. Go home and think about the purchase for at least 24 hours. If you are married, talk it over with your spouse. Often you will find that the need was not as great as you originally thought or other needs may be more important. Avoid impulse buying.

Waiting is even more beneficial for high-end electronic items. Consider how much laptop computers, MP3 players, and flat-screen televisions have come down in price. Avoid being an early adopter of this technology—you can save money and see what new advances occur in the technology.

9. **Buy quality.** This may sound strange in light of all the previous advice in this appendix. Whenever you buy, buy the best quality you can afford—especially when buying used. You can sometimes even get items you could not afford had you bought them new. One of the best examples of quality in buying used is clothing. Not only can you buy used clothing for very low prices, but after normal use, you may be able to resell them again at the price you originally paid. Of course, you won't always pay the lowest price. Service and convenience may be more important than price on occasion.

10. **Stockpile or anticipate needs.** Buy in quantity when going to the grocery store or to the membership warehouse to take advantage of quantity discounts. If a store is having a year-

end clearance on items such as tennis shoes, shirts, or pants, consider buying more than one. They may not fit your children initially, but sooner or later one child will grow into them. If not, you can use the new clothing as a gift.

11. **Prepurchased gifts.** How many gift occasions do you or your spouse or your children get invited to? If you're like us, the larger your circle of friends and family grows, the more baby showers, birthday parties, and anniversary parties you are invited to. Keep a closet full of gift inventory items that you bought on sale or at the end of the season to supply those last-minute or future gift needs.

12. **Babysitting co-op.** Get together with other couples you know in your area to develop a babysitting plan, trading time on a child-per-child basis. This will provide quality care without the expense. We've heard from people who estimate that in one year they saved over $300 by using their babysitting co-op, and they developed stronger friendships as well.

13. **Coupons.** Several grocery store chains in our areas offer double coupons. Even if none in your area do, grocery coupons can save you a great deal of money every week. It takes some work to clip the coupons, but it's well worth the trouble. Why not make coupon clipping a family affair?

Many Web sites allow you to electronically "clip" coupons. Check out www.coolsavings.com, www.couponcabin.com, www.coupons.com, or www.couponmom.com. (By the way, most of these sites offer coupons on other products and services you need for your home.) You can also go directly to the sites of major grocery chains such as Kroger or Safeway and see about special offers, especially for the shopper card members.

Another area in which coupons can benefit a family is in eating out. Don't feel guilty about using those two-for-one coupons—the restaurant is still making money. Often civic or nonprofit organizations sell coupon books containing hundreds of coupons such as two-for-one restaurant offers or 10 percent off your purchase at various stores. You might even keep one in each car plus one at home. If you are unexpectedly away from home at mealtime, you are not forced to pay full price at the local fast-food place—you can just pull the book out of the glove compartment and use a coupon.

14. **"You have not because you ask not," so negotiate.** We are great believers in negotiating price. Let's say you've done your research and are interested in purchasing a particular charcoal grill with a hefty price tag. After the salesperson explains all the features to you, ask him or her the simple question, "Is that price the best you can give?" Often, he or she will express a willingness to work with you. More than likely, you can negotiate 10 percent or more off the price— and the salesperson may even compliment you for asking.

We want to emphasize that we are not good negotiators when it comes to talking terms with salesmen. They are the pros, and we are amateurs. But we have found that the simple principle, "you have not because you ask not," really holds true. We do not negotiate hard; we simply ask if that is their best price. (As you may realize, this approach doesn't work so well with the large discount stores. It works better for smaller, locally owned stores when you're talking to a manager or owner.)

15. **Pay promptly.** After negotiating, do everything possible to fulfill your part of the bargain. That usually means paying in cash because that is what most merchants prefer. Pay your bills when due—don't try to extend the payment terms. If the merchant has been flexible, then you need to do everything you can to live up to your part of the bargain, which usually involves paying promptly. And that only builds goodwill with the merchant.

16. **Save on gas.** Get a rebate. Many gas stations offer their own credit cards with a rebate of 3 to 5 percent at their locations. Compare gas prices online before you leave home; www.gasbuddy.com will give you gas stations with the lowest prices on your commuting or trip route. (Of course, it won't make sense to drive too far out of your way to save two cents a gallon.)

    To improve gas mileage, keep the tires inflated, the air filter clean, and the car regularly maintained. Don't believe the various gas-saving claims of accessories and add-ons. The U.S. EPA tests reveal that most of these gadgets at auto supply stores don't work as promised.

    For even bigger savings on gas, carpool or ride-share. Web sites such as www.erideshare.com can hook you up with other drivers.

17. **Hold garage sales.** An annual garage sale can earn you money and help you get rid of stuff you normally would just keep accumulating. Frankly, it's unbelievable what people will buy at garage sales. These events can be fun. Involve the kids selling lemonade, and enjoy a spring Saturday where you can sit out in the sun and the fresh air and meet new people. We know of people who offer free Christian tracts and books. You won't get rich, but clearing out excess stuff and making a few hundred dollars feels good. You can often join in with your neighbors, and it's a great time to get to know them better as well.

18. **Give stuff away.** Why buy more storage containers, build a bigger garage, expand your attic, or add a storage building in your backyard? Get rid of unused items instead. We've been blessed when we have given away our clothes, food, used items, or occasionally furniture to people who need them. We are convinced that one of the reasons we seem to be blessed is because of our availability to share what the Lord has given us with others. Many veterans organizations will

pick up donations at your home; Goodwill and other charitable thrift shops have many drop-off locations.

19. **Dental schools.** Your company may not provide dental insurance, and the cost of preventative dental care can be expensive. If your county or state has a dental college or hygienist school, you may be able to get your teeth or your children's teeth cleaned at a considerable savings. These hygienists in training are supervised by a dentist and treat your children's teeth methodically. For an average cost of $10 to $15 per child, children can get their teeth cleaned, as well as get a fluoride treatment, sealant, and X rays if necessary. On top of that, they also get a new toothbrush. The clinic is grateful for having the children's teeth to work on—and you can be grateful for the money saved.

20. **Vaccinations.** The good news is that medicine has developed vaccines for many of the childhood diseases that plagued you and me. The bad news is these vaccination costs can add up. However, your county health department will probably inoculate against all major diseases free of charge or for a nominal fee. As a taxpayer, why shouldn't you consider taking advantage of this service? (Remember to keep your records and share them with your regular doctor.)

21. **Medicine/generic drugs.** Shop generic for basic medical items like aspirin and vitamins. Whether it means buying the local drugstore's house brand over-the-counter medication or getting your antihistamine prescription filled via a mail-order pharmacy, you rarely need to pay top dollar for a brand-name drug. For a typical generic children's antihistamine/decongestant, you can pay as little as one-quarter the price of a popular name brand—and the formula is exactly the same.

22. **Employee benefits.** It pays to carefully review the benefits available to you through your employer. These may include matching contributions to your 401(k), employee discounts,

and tuition reimbursement. In addition, you may benefit by participating in a flexible spending account (FSA)
through your employer. These plans allow employees to set
aside pretax income that can be used for qualifying expenses
like medical deductibles and child care. (One caution about
FSAs: you lose any unused money in your account at the
end of the year, so plan wisely.)

23. **Matching price policy.** Most retailers in our geographical
    areas will match or beat any advertised price. In the course
    of a year we will take advantage of this policy several times.
    Why drive all the way across town for an advertised sale item
    at a discount store if your full-service retailer down the street
    will match prices? Your local hardware store, for instance,
    may be more than happy to match the prices of a discount
    store when you provide a copy of the other store's ad. In
    fact, the hardware store is likely to be very appreciative of
    your patronage.

24. **Avoid recreational shopping.** Do you prowl the malls just
    for the fun of it? Do you dress up and even wear new outfits
    to the mall? When you are bored, do you watch the Home
    Shopping Network? Do you have a "Shop till You Drop"
    bumper sticker? We have spent enough time in financial
    counseling sessions to know that people often are not ratio-
    nal when they make purchasing decisions. Recreational
    shopping will lead you to buy items that you normally
    wouldn't. After all, if you spend three hours in the mall,
    shouldn't you buy a little something? Shopping is like any
    other temptation. If you can't handle it, flee from it. Don't
    put yourself in circumstances that will cater to your poten-
    tial weaknesses. If you're going shopping, know exactly what
    you're going for, make a list, and don't deviate from it.

25. **Libraries.** Rather than buy books or rent the latest movie,
    become a faithful user of your neighborhood library. Librar-

ies today loan audiobooks, videos, and DVDs. They also provide Internet access, have story hours, provide meeting rooms, and are a great environment for your children to spend time in. Besides saving you money, libraries are a great way to instill in your children the love of reading, which will benefit them throughout their lives.

26. **Repair vs. replacement.** America has a "newer model–throw it away" mentality. For electronic and computer items, this is usually appropriate due to technology changes and the general decline in prices over time. For other ones, usually big-ticket items such as cars and furniture, repairing is generally better. If you're preparing for the arrival of the third baby and the twice-used bassinet looks worn, consider painting it and getting a new mattress cover. It will look almost as good as new. The point is, don't be quick to think you need a new item. Perhaps the old one can be repaired. Reupholstering furniture is another way you may be able to save. Often a reupholstered piece is better than new because the craftsman has repaired and reinforced structural components and probably used better materials than those used in the piece's original construction.

27. **Seasonal buying.** In these days of perpetual sales and "discounts off suggested list price," who knows what a real sale is. In the midst of the confusion, however, there are traditional sale periods when it pays to plan your purchases. For example, many stores clear out their old lines of furniture and replace them with the new year's merchandise right after Christmas. After-Christmas white sales provide an excellent time to stock up on linens. You can save on kids' clothing by buying them one season in advance.

The best time to buy a car is in the fall when the model year changes. May and June are not good times to buy a convertible, used or new.

28. **Haircuts.** Some families send their five-year-olds to stylists for $20 haircuts. That money could be put to better use. Hair-salon chains usually charge less than other hairstylists, and you can often save even more by using their coupons. Or get reduced-rate cuts at a local beauty school, particularly for the men in the family. For even greater savings, buy electric clippers at a discount department store and have a family haircutting night.

29. **Birthday parties.** Over the years, my (Ron's) children were invited to some birthday extravaganzas. One family rented a roller-skating rink for an entire afternoon. Another held a party at a karate studio with instructors present. Yet another family had a party in their home in which the birthday child's older brothers did a magic show. Guess which party my children enjoyed most? The home magic show! We found that good old-fashioned birthday parties are often the most fun, and we don't have to get into the one-upmanship race. Treasure hunts, pin the tail on the donkey—all of the old favorites still work, and most kids have fun at these parties. Visit www.birthdaypartyideas.com for additional ideas on do-it-yourself parties.

30. **Envelopes.** There are a few areas in which even our natural bent toward saving needs a bit of external control. We always recommend a budget for people, but if you're one of those who can't stand a spending plan, try a "partial budget." For example, many people have a hard time controlling how much money they spend eating out in restaurants and fast-food establishments. If this is an area you would like to control but haven't yet set up a formal budget, simply begin each month by placing the amount you want to spend eating out in an envelope, and when the envelope is empty, stop spending. This time-tested method will save you money in the areas of most concern without causing you to come up with a formal budget.

31. **Cooking in advance.** This suggestion can prove a lifesaver, especially now that most families have microwaves. Keep some frozen meals on hand by making double batches of recipes like lasagna and freezing half of them. That way, on a day when your schedules are hectic, you'll have a premade meal ready to serve. You'll enjoy a hearty, nutritious meal in minutes instead of expensive and less-nutritious fast food.

32. **Plant a vegetable or flower garden.** This healthy idea may help trim food bills, particularly if you plant food items that are more expensive at the stores. Cutting fresh flowers for your table or as a gift to others costs much less than paying a florist.

33. **Change your eating habits.** Drink water rather than soft drinks and cut out the impulse snack items at the vending machine. Plan ahead and put an apple in your briefcase rather than a prepackaged food. Keep a jar of peanuts in the car to snack on while running errands. Cook at home rather than going out. Surprisingly, eating healthier usually means eating cheaper.

34. **Trim your utility bills by monitoring usage.** Consider lowering your thermostat and dressing in layers in the winter. You can purchase programmable thermostats at most home improvement stores. You can set these devices to raise and lower the temperature of your house according to your lifestyle needs and schedules. Your electricity bills are likely to drop by 15 to 20 percent.

35. **Conduct a home energy audit.** Many utility companies offer a free home energy audit to help identify areas of savings. You can also search the Internet for common checklists to conduct your own audit. Ways to save energy include caulking around windows and doors, shutting off vents and doors to unused rooms, adding ventilation in the attic, and so on.

36. **Travel smart.** Time your vacations to coincide with off-peak rates, when the deals are better and the destinations less crowded. Use the power of Internet shopping comparisons among various travel Web sites.

37. **Consider relocating.** Although somewhat of a last resort to deal with rising housing costs, think about moving to a lower-cost area. With technology improvements, it's often possible to work from more remote locations or run a business from a smaller town rather than a metropolis. The cost difference between large cities, particularly those on the coasts of the United States, and rural areas is very significant.

38. **Go public with university choices.** If you or your child picks a highly rated public university over a private school, you will save $20,000 to $30,000 per year. Since a college education is typically as good as the student makes it, public institutions can provide a great value. Before selecting a private college, then, evaluate whether the quality is worth the cost difference.

39. **Eat lunch out rather than dinner.** Arrange your next date with that special someone over lunch rather than dinner. Get the same food with the same atmosphere for a much lower price and in a smaller crowd. It's easier to find a babysitter, and you'll sleep better at night if your stomach is not so full.

40. **Old-fashioned family fun.** There's a misconception in our society that if you don't spend money for an activity, it can't possibly be fun. Indeed, we Americans are very good at creating sensory experiences, usually expensive ones, to entertain ourselves. We venture to say that most of these experiences do not build memories. The good old-fashioned activities like family picnics, board game nights, walks, games of catch, and sports activities are what the kids really appreciate. A great way to retain these memories is in a family scrapbook. Relive your family vacations each year, and as time

goes by some of those humorous incidents will get funnier and funnier.

## Create Your Own Money-Saving Tips

Most people do not have an income problem but rather a spending problem. We trust these tips have been helpful and will spur you into some creative thinking on how you can save money in your own situation. What works for us may not work for you, but all of us can save money in certain areas without sacrificing much time, perhaps even improving the quality of life.

As you can see, saving money takes work, but the more you work at it, the easier it becomes. It tends to become more of a habit and a mind-set. Being careful with your expenses ultimately allows you to do the things that you really want to do—such as going out on more dates with your spouse.

On a final note, we advise you not to try squeezing every penny out of every dollar or make saving money into some kind of "second religion." Our families try to be good stewards not so we have more *money* but more *freedom*—the freedom to give to people with needs, the freedom to be flexible in our budgets, the freedom to be spontaneous in our spending without compromising our overall financial plans. Balance is the key. We may save money on the spending side, but that gives us freedom in other areas.

# NOTES

1. Jason Hanna, "Their House Survived Ike, but It's the Only One Left," *CNN.com*, September 19, 2008, http://edition.cnn.com/2008/US/09/18/ike.last.house.standing/; Juan A. Lozano, "Texas Residents of Ravaged Peninsula Head Home," *USA Today*, September 27, 2008, http://www.usatoday.com/weather/storms/hurricanes/2008-09-26-ike-bolivar-peninsula_N.htm.

2. Susan Buchanan, "Coffee Retailers Endure Economic Storm," *Wall Street Journal*, July 28, 2008.

3. Janet Adamy, "As Starbucks Retrenches, a Loss Stings," *Wall Street Journal*, July 31, 2008.

4. Gary McWilliams, "U.S. Consumers Trade Down as Economic Angst Grows," *Wall Street Journal*, July 11, 2008.

5. Lovie Smith, who had served as an assistant coach under Dungy in Tampa Bay, wrote the Time 100 entry for Dungy. Smith coaches the Chicago Bears, the team that lost to the Colts in Super Bowl XLI. Read Smith's tribute at http://www.time.com/time/specials/2007/time100/article/0,28804,1595326_1615754_1615744,00.html.

6. Tony Dungy, *Quiet Strength* (Carol Stream, IL: Tyndale House, 2007), 16.

7. Bruce Horovitz, "Financial Fears Send Nation's Stress Soaring," *USA Today*, September 28, 2008, http://www.usatoday.com/money/economy/income/2008-09-25-stress-bailout-recession_N.htm.

8. Ibid.

9. College Board, "Tuition Increases Continue to Slow at Public Colleges According to the College Board's 2006 Reports on College Pricing and Financial Aid," October 24, 2006, http://www.collegeboard.com/press/releases/150634.html.

10. U.S. Social Security Administration, Office of Policy, Monthly Statistical Snapshot, September 2008, http://www.ssa.gov/policy/docs/quickfacts/stat_snapshot/index.html (accessed October 30, 2008).

11. Lewis Grizzard, *Atlanta Journal*, June 24, 1990.

12. Proverbs 27:23 (NKJV) admonishes us to "be diligent to know the state of your flocks, and attend to your herds." Most of us don't have livestock to track, but the principle is know what you own.

13. Ipsos Public Affairs conducted the survey for ING U.S. Financial Services of Atlanta of 1,000 U.S. adults in late 2007 and early 2008. Report details found in Sue Asci, "Financial Fear Factors," *InvestmentNews*, May 26, 2008, 30.

14. Mark H. McCormack, *What They Don't Teach You at Harvard Business School: Notes from a Street-Smart Executive* (New York: Bantam Books, 1984).

15. Steve Hamm, "The New Age of Frugality," *BusinessWeek*, October 9, 2008, http://www.businessweek.com/magazine/content/08_42/b4104054847273.htm?chan=top+news_top+news+index+-+temp_top+story.

16. Thomas J. Stanley and William D. Danko, *The Millionaire Next Door: The Surprising Secrets of America's Wealthy* (New York: Simon and Schuster, 1996), 10.

17. Ibid., 49.

18. Ibid., 37.

19. Ibid., 33.

20. Survey by the American Enterprise Institute for Public Policy Research in Washington as published in *InvestmentNews*, February 26, 2007, 1.

21. Juliet Chung, "Ancient Collections," *Wall Street Journal*, September 20–21, 2008.

22. The Nilson Report, as cited in Ben Woolsey and Matt Schulz, "Credit Card Industry Facts, Debt Statistics 2006–2008," http://www.creditcards.com/credit-card-news/credit-card-industry-facts-personal-debt-statistics-1276.php (accessed September 25, 2008).

23. Obtained from tax statistics accessed at www.irs.gov. Table 2.1, "Returns with Itemized Deductions: Sources of Income, Adjustments, Itemized Deductions by Type, Exemptions, and Tax Items, by Size of Adjusted Gross Income, Tax Year 2006."

24. Part of headline for article by Susanne Craig, Jeffrey McCracken, Jon Hilsenrath, and Deborah Solomon, September 16, 2008.

25. Headline for article by Matthew Karnitschnig, Deborah Solomon, and Liam Pleven, September 17, 2008.

26. Headline for article by Tom Lauricella, Liz Rappaport, and Annelena Lobb, September 18, 2008.

27. Headline for article by Jon Hilsenrath, Serena Ng, and Damian Paletta, September 18, 2008.

28. Headline for article by David Wessel, September 20–21, 2008.

29. E. S. Browning and Annelena Lobb, "Dow Jumps Another 358.75 Points, Ends Wild Week Nearly Unchanged," *Wall Street Journal*, September 20–21, 2008.

30. The term *fiscalosophy* was coined by Mitch Anthony, the founder and president of Advisor Insights, Inc. He also writes the column "Financial Life Planning" for *Financial Advisor* magazine.

31. Jilian Mincer, "Why It's Wrong to Hold Too Much of One Stock," *Wall Street Journal*, September 4, 2008.

# ABOUT THE AUTHORS

**RON BLUE** has been a financial planner and consultant for more than 40 years. In 1979, he founded a financial planning firm because of his conviction that Christians would handle their personal finances better if they were counseled objectively with the highest technical expertise from a biblical perspective. That firm grew to manage over $2 billion in assets for more than 5,000 clients nationwide.

Ron now serves as president of Kingdom Advisors. This organization is an international effort to equip and motivate Christian financial professionals to communicate biblical wisdom in their lives and practices, resulting in financial freedom and increased giving to Christian ministries around the world.

Ron is the author of 16 books on personal finances from a biblical perspective, including the best seller *Master Your Money*. His other books include *Generous Living*, *Your Money after the Big 5-0* (coauthored with Larry Burkett), *Splitting Heirs*, *Your Kids Can Master Their Money*, and *Faith-Based Family Finances*.

**JEREMY WHITE** has been a certified public accountant since 1988, with financial experience in public accounting and industry. He is a partner with Blythe, White & Associates, a certified public accounting and consulting firm in Paducah, Kentucky. He is a Kingdom Advisors Qualified Member. Jeremy has coauthored or assisted with five other best-selling financial books. These include *The New Master Your Money*, *Splitting Heirs*, and *Your Kids Can Master Their Money*. Along with Ron Blue and the late Larry Burkett, he also wrote *Your Money after the Big 5-0*. He also assisted Ron Blue with writing *Faith-Based Family Finances*.

# HOW WOULD YOU LIKE ACCESS TO YOUR OWN FINANCIAL ADVISOR 24-7?

## THIS BOOK IS THE NEXT BEST THING.

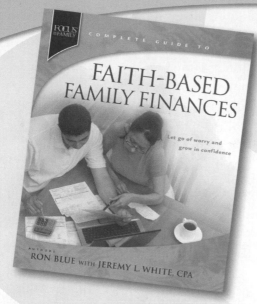

Whether you're a financial whiz, a financial novice, or somewhere in between, *Faith-Based Family Finances* is filled with commonsense, practical tools to help you make wise financial decisions year after year. By following this financial blueprint, you will lay a solid foundation for fiscal health in every stage of life and add strong money management tools to your repertoire. In each chapter, you'll read stories of people who struggle with the same money issues that you do—and the solutions that helped them overcome their challenges.

You'll find answers to questions such as:
- How can I honor God in the way I deal with money?
- How do I live within my means?
- How can we dig ourselves out of all this debt?
- Should we buy a home or continue to rent?
- How can my spouse and I stop arguing over money?
- What options do we have to save for our kids' college expenses?
- How do I know if I'm making a wise investment decision?
- Will I have enough to live on when I get older?
- How do we decide how much—and where—to donate?
- What are the critical components of a will?

*Faith-Based Family Finances*: A biblical understanding of money management that helps you let go of worry and grow in confidence.

# MasterYourMoney.com

A FREE RESOURCE FOR BIBLICAL FINANCIAL DECISION MAKING

Ron Blue is uniquely suited to be a voice of clarity and confidence for your financial decisions. With more than 40 years of experience in the financial services industry and having authored more than 15 books on personal finance from a biblical perspective, Ron speaks with experience, integrity, and perspective. His insight into financial decision making is grounded in biblical wisdom and has been tested over time in the lives of thousands he has touched. Ron's professional expertise and faith journey are integrated into all of his advice and counsel.

- Watch Q and A video of Ron as he answers frequently asked questions about your finances.
- Learn about the process of creating your own financial plan that is in line with your financial priorities.
- Discover more about scriptural teaching on stewardship and decision making.
- Access biblically based advice developed over Ron's 40 years in the financial services industry.
- Understand the 11 uses of money so that you can have peace in your financial decisions.

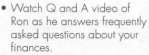

www.MasterYourMoney.com

# KINGDOM ✦ ADVISORS
## *Qualified*

## Choose Wisely™

Kingdom Advisors, founded by Larry Burkett and led by Ron Blue, exists to engage, equip, and empower Christian financial advisors to communicate biblical wisdom to their clients, apply professional principles in their practices, and live out their faith in their marketplace for Kingdom impact.

As part of that mission, Kingdom Advisors has created the Qualified Kingdom Advisor™ designation to provide assurance that a particular advisor has participated in the Kingdom Advisors education program, has agreed to Kingdom Advisors' ethics requirements, and has committed to incorporating biblical wisdom into his or her financial advice. The financial advisors eligible to seek the Qualified Kingdom Advisor™ designation include those in the core financial disciplines, including financial planners, investment professionals, attorneys, accountant/ tax professionals, insurance professionals, and mortgage professionals.

Your financial advisor's worldview is of critical importance because ultimately, all good financial advice has its root in biblical wisdom. Only a Christian financial advisor equipped to deliver biblical wisdom can offer advice and counsel consistent with the values and priorities of a believer. Our goal at Kingdom Advisors is twofold, both to equip Christian financial advisors to integrate that biblical wisdom with their financial counsel and to provide you with confidence in your search for such a financial advisor by designating those advisors who have met our criteria and completed our training as Qualified Kingdom Advisors™.

Yours in Christ,

*Ron Blue*

Ron Blue

Kindgom Advisors • 5605 Glenridge Drive., #450 • Atlanta, GA 30342 • 404-497-7680

www.KingdomAdvisors.org

# FOCUS ON THE FAMILY®

## *Welcome to the family!*

**W**hether you purchased this book, borrowed it, or received it as a gift, we're glad you're reading it. It's just one of the many helpful, encouraging, and biblically based resources produced by Focus on the Family for people in all stages of life.

Focus began in 1977 with the vision of one man, Dr. James Dobson, a licensed psychologist and author of numerous best-selling books on marriage, parenting, and family. Alarmed by the societal, political, and economic pressures that were threatening the existence of the American family, Dr. Dobson founded Focus on the Family with one employee and a once-a-week radio broadcast aired on 36 stations.

Now an international organization reaching millions of people daily, Focus on the Family is dedicated to preserving values and strengthening and encouraging families through the life-changing message of Jesus Christ.

------------------------------------------------

### Focus on the Family Magazines

These faith-building, character-developing publications address the interests, issues, concerns, and challenges faced by every member of your family from preschool through the senior years.

| Focus on the Family **Citizen®** U.S. news issues | Focus on the Family **Clubhouse Jr.™** Ages 4 to 8 | Focus on the Family **Clubhouse™** Ages 8 to 12 | **Breakaway®** Teen guys | **Brio®** Teen girls 12 to 16 | **Brio & Beyond®** Teen girls 16 to 19 | **Plugged In®** Reviews movies, music, TV |

---

**FOR MORE INFORMATION**

 **Online:**
Log on to www.family.org
In Canada, log on to
www.focusonthefamily.ca

 **Phone:**
Call toll free: (800) A-FAMILY
In Canada, call toll free:
(800) 661-9800